JOURNEY DOWN THE YEARS

Ruskin Bond has been writing for over sixty years, and now has over 120 titles in print—novels, collections of short stories, poetry, essays, anthologies and books for children. His first novel, *The Room on the Roof*, received the prestigious John Llewellyn Rhys Prize in 1957. He has also received the Padma Shri (1999), the Padma Bhushan (2014) and two awards from Sahitya Akademi—one for his short stories and another for his writings for children. In 2012, the Delhi government gave him its Lifetime Achievement Award.

Born in 1934, Ruskin Bond grew up in Jamnagar, Shimla, New Delhi and Dehradun. Apart from three years in the UK, he has spent all his life in India, and now lives in Mussoorie with his adopted family.

By the same author

- A Little Book of Friendship
- A Little Book of Life
- A Little Night Music
- A Long Walk for Bina (Illustrated)
- A Mussoorie Mystery
- A Song of Many Rivers
- All Roads Lead to Ganga
- Angry River (Illustrated)
- Falling in Love Again
- Funny Side Up
- Ghost Stories From the Raj
- Great Stories for Children
- Hanuman to the Rescue (Illustrated)
- Monkey Trouble and Other Grandfather Stories
- My Favourite Nature Stories
- No Man Is An Island
- Once Upon A Time in the Doon
- Party Time in Mussoorie
- Roads to Mussoorie
- Romi and the Wildfire (Illustrated)
- Ruskin Bond's Children's Omnibus
- School Days
- School Times
- Stories Short and Sweet (Illustrated)
- Strange Men Strange Places
- Tales and Legends From India
- The Beast Tamer
- The Big Book of Animal Stories
- The Blue Umbrella (Illustrated)
- The Children's Companion
- The Elephant and the Cassowary
- The Empty House
- The Essential Collection for Young Readers
- The India I Love
- The Jungle Omnibus
- The Kipling Road
- The Lagoon
- The Laughing Skull
- The Perfect Murder
- The Prospects of Flowers
- The Regimental Myna
- The Road to the Bazaar
- The Rupa Book of Great Suspense Stories
- The Rupa Book of Haunted Houses
- The Rupa Book of Heartwarming Stories
- The Rupa Book of Ruskin Bond's Himalayan Tales
- The Rupa Book of Scary Stories
- The Rupa Book of Shikar Stories
- The Rupa Book of Snappy Surprises
- The Rupa Book of Travellers' Tales
- The Rupa Book of Wicked Stories
- The Rupa Laughter Omnibus
- The Ruskin Bond Horror Omnibus
- The Ruskin Bond Mini Bus
- The Very Best of Ruskin Bond
- The Whistling Schoolboy and Other Stories of School Life
- The White Tiger and Other Stories
- The Wise Parrot
- The World Outside My Window
- Tigers for Dinner
- Too Much Trouble
- Voting at Fosterganj
- White Clouds, Green Mountains
- Who Kissed Me in the Dark

RUSKIN BOND
JOURNEY DOWN THE YEARS

RUPA

Published by
Rupa Publications India Pvt. Ltd 2017
7/16, Ansari Road, Daryaganj
New Delhi 110002

Sales centres:
Allahabad Bengaluru Chennai
Hyderabad Jaipur Kathmandu
Kolkata Mumbai

Copyright © Ruskin Bond 2017

The views and opinions expressed in this book are the author's own and the facts are as reported by him which have been verified to the extent possible, and the publishers are not in any way liable for the same.

All rights reserved.
No part of this publication may be reproduced, transmitted, or stored in a retrieval system, in any form or by any means, electronic, mechanical, photocopying, recording or otherwise, without the prior permission of the publisher.

ISBN: 978-81-291-4740-0

First impression 2017

10 9 8 7 6 5 4 3 2 1

Printed at Replika Press Pvt. Ltd, India

This book is sold subject to the condition that it shall not, by way of trade or otherwise, be lent, resold, hired out, or otherwise circulated, without the publisher's prior consent, in any form of binding or cover other than that in which it is published.

Contents

Author's Note   *vii*

1. Journey Down the Years   1
2. My Adventure Wind   7
3. My Two Years in London   12
4. My Limehouse Adventure   23
5. Journey to Mathura   28
6. The Taj at High Noon   33
7. The Gallery of Birds   38
8. The Charming Bloodsucker   43
9. Gentle Shade by Day   47

10. Gran's Kitchen	50
11. A Book Lover's Life-Long Hunt	55
12. Those Fragrant Moments	59
13. Wayside Stations and Platforms	63
14. Mountains in My Blood	68
15. The Last Walnut	71
16. The Vanishing Trees	74
17. The Tenacity of Mountain Water	78
18. The Trees are My Brothers	82
19. Petals on the Ganga	86
20. Wild Flowers near a Mountain Stream	91
21. Of Rivers and Pilgrims	95
22. The Joy of Water	101
23. Sounds I Like to Hear	104
24. Guests Who Fly in from the Forest	109
25. In Search of a Winter Garden	114

Author's Note

Over the years I think I have enjoyed all my writing, except when I have been given a deadline or asked to write on a specific subject. Then it becomes a task, like having to write a school essay within a limited amount of time and on a limited range of subjects.

It's wonderful to have the freedom to write on anything that has taken one's fancy—whether it be a crow on a chamber, an old lady in a walnut tree, a sleepy afternoon at the Taj, Lord Krishna's peacocks near Mathura, and the fragrance of petunias and sweet peas.

Sometime ago, while going through a drawer of old

cuttings and manuscripts, I came across some of my old favourites—many of them unknown to my regular readers—and I put them together to form a little collection of journeys remembered and fragrances never forgotten, interspersing these with a few recent offering such as 'My Adventure Wind' and 'The Trees are My Brother', and I hope the resultant potpourri will please the reader with a fragrance all its own.

Ruskin Bond

Landour, Mussoorie
March 2017

Journey Down the Years

As a novelist and storyteller, I have always drawn upon my memories of places that I have known and lived in over the years. More than most writers, perhaps, I find myself drawing inspiration from the past—my childhood, adolescence, youth, early manhood...

It is over sixty years since I wrote my first novel, *The Room on the Roof*, the story of a sixteen-year-old on a journey of self-discovery in small-town India—chiefly Dehradun.

But to talk of my early inspiration I must go back to my very beginnings, to the then small, princely state of

Jamnagar, tucked away in the Gulf of Kutch. Here my father started a small palace school for the princesses, and I learnt to read and write along with them. I was there till the age of six, and I still treasure vivid memories of Jamnagar's beautiful palaces and sandy beaches. Some of these landmarks are preserved for me in photographs taken by my father, which I have to this day. An old palace with pretty windows of coloured glass remained fixed in my memory and many years later gave me the story 'The Room of Many Colours', which also inspired an episode in a TV serial called *Ek Tha Rusty*, in which that wonderful old thespian, Zohra Sehgal, excelled in the role of an eccentric, albeit fictional rani.

The first book I read by myself was *Alice in Wonderland*, and it might well have been set in the palace gardens—rose bushes, privet hedges and croquet lawns, all at hand! But this fairytale world disappeared from my life forever when World War II broke out and my father joined the Royal Air Force. I spent a memorable year and a half with him in New Delhi, then still a very new city—just the capital area designed by Edwin Lutyens and Connaught Place, with its gleaming new shops and restaurants and cinemas. We had to walk through scrub jungles to get to Humayun's Tomb; take a tonga to get to the railway station at the other end of Old Delhi; keep cool with table fans and khus-khus matting well-soaked by the bhisti or water carrier, who came around at regular intervals. I saw Laurel and Hardy films and devoured milkshakes at the Keventers Milk Bar, even as the Quit India Movement gathered momentum.

I was seven years old and yet to go to a proper school. I would have been quite happy to never go to one, but my father took me to Simla (now Shimla) and put me in Bishop Cotton. While the best thing about Simla was the mountain railway, the best thing about the school was the library. School life did not inspire much of my writing, but that well-stocked library gave me a solid grounding in the classics and the literature of the time.

I was barely ten when I received the news of my father's death, and my life was turned upside down for some time. I had to adjust to my stepfather's Punjabi home in Dehradun, and that took a little doing, as his main interests were shikar and second-hand cars. But Dehradun at the time was a pretty little town of some 40,000 inhabitants; today it is a state capital with a population nearing 17 lakh in number. These days, the lychee gardens have given way to blocks of flats. But the old Dehra, with its country lanes and rolling hills, found its way into many of my stories.

When I was seventeen, I was shipped off to the UK to 'better my prospects' as my mother put it. Out of a longing for India and the friends I had made in Dehra came my first novel—*The Room on the Roof*—featuring the life and loves of Rusty, my alter ego. Two years and two drafts later it found a publisher, André Deutsch, who would later introduce V.S. Naipaul to the literary world. In those days, the standard advance was just £50—but it was enough to bring me back to India.

In the 1950s everyone travelled by sea, as air services were still in their infancy. A passenger liner took about three weeks from Southampton to Bombay (now Mumbai), stopping for a day or two at Gibraltar, Port Said, Aden and Karachi. After docking in Bombay, I took a train to Dehra, where I stepped onto the platform of the small railway station and embarked on the hazardous journey of a freelance writer.

Railway stations! Trains! Platforms! I knew as long as these were there I would never run out of stories. Ambala Junction gave me *The Woman on Platform8*, the Kalka-Shimla Railway route gave me *The Tunnel*, and a small wayside halt on the fringe of the Siwalik forests gave me *The Night Train at Deoli*.

In the 1950s trains still used steam engines, and there was a certain romance attached to train journeys, a romance that was captured by Rudyard Kipling in *Kim* and many of his short stories. It is over 130 years since A.H. Wheeler & Co. started their chain of railway bookstalls, and published many of Kipling's early stories (written in the 1880s when he was a journalist with *The Civil and Military Gazette*) in their Indian Railway Library series—collectors' items today.

I did not have Wheeler's or *The Gazette*, but I had publications like *Sainik Samachar*, *Sport and Pastime*, *Shankar's Weekly*, *The Leader*, *The Statesman*, *Illustrated Weekly* and others—all willing to pay a budding young writer anything from ₹25 to ₹50 for a short story. I wrote for anyone who would publish me, and I had great fun eking out a living for a few years.

Those small cheques enabled me to live off dhaba food, but what I badly needed was home cooking, so I ended up in Delhi, where my mother was living. There I looked for inspiration in tombs and monuments and the ever-expanding city, but did not find it, and my productivity dropped. Then came an excursion to Shahjahanpur, my father's birthplace, where the old cantonment hadn't changed since 1857—providing me with the background for *A Flight of Pigeons*, the mutiny story that was to be filmed later by Shyam Benegal, called *Junoon*. It had been recommended by legendary Urdu writer Ismat Chughtai, who also took a small role in the film.

Escape from Delhi had become a priority for me. I felt drawn to the hills above Dehra. On the outskirts of Mussoorie I found a small cottage, surrounded by oak and maple trees where the rent, thankfully, was nominal.

Since then my forty-five years in Mussoorie have been an epic in themselves, and have already filled several books. I do go away sometimes—to Delhi, Orissa, Rajasthan—but I always return in some haste to my small study with its window looking out upon the mountains and the valley. I'm of the opinion that every writer needs a window. Preferably two.

Is the house, the room, the situation...important for a writer? A good wordsmith should be able to work anywhere—in a moving train, in a hotel room, on board a ship struggling against a typhoon, or under an erupting volcano. But to me, the room you live in day after day is all-important.

The stories and the poems float in through my window, float in from the magic mountains, and the words appear on the page without much effort on my part. I can see the curvature of the earth from my window, because there is nothing between me and the far horizon. Planet Earth belongs to me. And at night, the stars are almost within reach.

My Adventure Wind

That's what I called it when I was a boy. A wind that sprang up unexpectedly, bringing me to life, reviving me if I was in the dumps.

I remember the first time I gave it a name. I was twelve, sitting with a friend on a bench at the far end of the school's first flat, facing the Tara Devi hill across the wide valley. The air was very still, and my friend Omar and I were equally still, not knowing what to do with ourselves during the twenty-minute break before supper.

Then this wind appeared from nowhere, as it does sometimes in the Himalayan foothills. It ruffled my hair, made my eyes sting a little, lifted the football scarf from my shoulders. I looked at Omar. He was unruffled. He had thick black hair and he used brylcreem cream. No wind could affect it!

'This wind,' I said, 'Doesn't it make you feel adventurous?'

'It makes me feel cold,' he said, 'Let's go inside. It's almost supper-time.'

'It makes me feel adventurous,' I said, 'I want to run about. I want to fly!'

'Well, don't fly here. It's a big drop to the next flat, and you'll only break your neck. Lets' run as fast as we can to the dininghall. That way we'll be first in line for supper.'

So we raced across the flat, but on an impulse I took a right turn, and ended up, breathless, just inside the school gate, which had just been closed for the night. I was tempted to climb the gate and escape into the darkness, but I wasn't really thinking of running away from school, all I wanted was a little freedom. So I stood there under the deodars, and the wind that had brought me there now made its presence felt high up in the tree with a who-whoo-whooo, a strange humming sound unique to the branches of this particular kind of tree.

The wind makes different sounds in different trees, as I was to discover over a period of time. In certain trees, a rustling sound; as in the oak and house-chestnuts. In the pines it whistles, in the deodar it hums. In the maples in the spring, it makes a sound like castanets. All different kinds of wind instruments, you might say.

In the plains the trees are different, and a strong wind will bend the tall eucalyptus and make it groan and sigh. The jacaranda and laburnum shred their petals silently, without resistance. The mango crackles as it loses a branch or two. An old, unsupported banyan tree comes down with a crash. Nothing can prevail against the wind once it has gathered strength and momentum.

From the age of seventeen to eighteen, I lived in the Channel Islands, between France and England. Almost every day was a windy day, and in winter they were gales, rushing across the sea and tossing small ships about. Standing on the crest of a hill, I could lean against the wind without falling over.

Late one evening, when the tide was in, I stood on the sea wall, enjoying the sound of the wind and the waves. And as the salt spray struck against my face, I knew it was my 'adventure' wind. It stirred something inside me, and I resolved to leave the island the very next day and see what life could offer me in London.

And this I did, much to the consternation of my aunt and uncle, who had opened their home to me. But I was eighteen and free and eager to make mistakes. And off I went.

My London days are another story. This is about the wind, my own personal wind, and it found me again many years later, when I made my home on this Himalayan range, open to wind and rain and brilliant sunshine.

'I have been looking for you all these years,' said the wind, as it came rushing up the hillside to take me in its arms and hold me in its loving embrace. It tousled my hair, kissed me on the lips and cheeks, fling my scarf away, and was so overpowering that I had to run home and lock the door against it.

And then it was at the windows, doing its best to get in.

'Let me in, let me in!' it shouted. Then the rain came and quelled it, and it went away sulking but promising to be back…

It came back the other night, bringing with it a heavy fall of snow. The windowpanes were thick with frost and ice. But a strong morning sun cleared this away, and the snow-covered hills were revealed in all their sublime splendour. Sublime splendour? I must learn not to use words in excess of their meaning. Just 'splendour' was sufficient! And more effective.

Anyway, the wind went away, leaving me with the snow and an irate milkman. He'd been ringing the bell for sometime, but of course there has been no electricity for two days and nights, so the bell wasn't working. And we had been without any news of the outside would, as there was no TV or newspaper delivery. Phoned Dolly in Amritsar and asked her to bring me up to date with the news. She told me that a certain minister's wife had been found dead in her hotel room under mysterious circumstances. Trust a woman to give me this choice little scandal. Whatever happened to the election campaign, Syria and the falling rupee? These through will pass, of course. And they cannot compete with a love triangle ending in tragedy. Especially, if it involves one of the country's ruling elite.

Day four, and still no electricity, except in the homes of the super-rich where generators have been installed. Now Bill can't use his electric blanket, and Beena can't recharge her cellphone. Hundreds of cellphones are useless, cannot be recharged. By some miracle, my old telephone, which is usually out of order, is working perfectly. In the hotel down the road there is no water and won't be, until the pumps start working. The Bank's computers aren't functioning. Back to the pen or the old typewriters!

Oh, for the life of a hill-station in mid-winter!

My Two Years in London

I was lonely in London.

Living alone in a big city, working in an office from nine to five, and coming back to a gas-fire in an empty bed-sitting room, was not what I wanted out of life. I'd go out to eat in a small café, then return to my room, put a sheet of paper into my small portable typewriter, and type out a page or two of my novel. It was into its second draft. And there would be a third before it finally found favour with its eventual publisher.

Diana Athill, my publisher's editor, was kind and helpful. The people in the Photax Office, where I

My Two Years in London

worked, were kind and friendly. My landlady was kind and solicitous. Or I should say landladies, because I had at least three of them, one after another—Belsize Park, Haverstock Hill, Swiss Cottage—all Jewish landladies, widows I think, who never troubled or scolded me if I came in late or played my radio too loudly. One of them gave me breakfast in my room. Scrambled eggs, occasionally with peppers. This helped sustain me, because for lunch—at a snackbar near the office—it was almost always baked beans on toast, the cheapest item on their menu.

People were kind,
But I was lonely,
I had no companions of my own age.

So I went to the pictures. And once a month to the theatre. And I dropped at Foyles and bought old books. And I came home to my empty room, lit the gas-fire and worked on my book.

After about six months on my own, I found I was losing vision in my right eye. It was as though I was looking at the world through a shifting cloud. I took vitamins, they had been 'discovered' only recently—and experimented with various eye-drops—but the cloud only got darker and denser. So I went to a doctor, who said it needed further investigation and got me admitted to the Hampstead General Hospital. There, various specialists came to see me. One said I was suffering from malnutrition; true enough. Another said I had rale's disease, a rare condition of the retina. A third felt it had something to do with a sluggish liver. (I'd suffered from jaundice in the past.) Tests showed that my intestines were full of amoebiasis, no doubt brought with me from India, and I was put on a course of emetine injections, which made me feel awful. Then my eye, or rather retina, was photographed by a high intensity camera, and the resultant picture appeared in a medical journal. (Not my picture, only the eye's; I had to wait a few years before my own mugshot appeared in a newspaper.

Once the amoeba had been vanquished, I (or rather my sick eye), was given cortisone injections, cortisone then being the wonder drug that was supposed to clear up all sorts of intractable conditions. This left my poor eye looking rather bloody and fierce, prompting one fellow patient to remark that I could have passed for *T Phantom of the Opera*.

Weakened by the emitine and various laxatives, I found myself too weak to even get up in order to visit the loo, so I was given the privilege of having a bed-pan. This occasioned some raillery from the others in the ward (it was a general ward with about twenty beds), who labelled me the B-P Superman—the Bed-pan Superman, after the British Petroleum Superman who was on all the hoardings.

I did improve rapidly, and was soon making the rounds of the ward, interviewing the other patients like a doctor on the rounds, quizzing them on their ailments and recommending purgatives and the bed-pan.

The book trolley came the rounds every day, and I read a book a day, discovering the stories of William Saroyan (*My Name is Aram* and *The Humans Comedy*), Denton Welch (*A Voice Through a Cloud*), and Josephine Tey (*The Daughter of Time*).

Saroyan had grown up in an Armenian immigrant community in California, and in his stories he captured the essence of small-town life in his part of the world. He won the Pulitzer Prize for his play, *The Time of Your Life*, and was very popular in the 1940s and '50s, but most of his work is now out of print.

Denton Welch was a promising young English writer who had a tragic accident while riding his bicycle on a country road. He was knocked down and run over by a lorry. For over a year, he lingered between life and death, and during this period he managed to write his very moving account of his struggle to recover. He succumbed to his many injuries. I hope *A Voice Through a Cloud* is reprinted some day. His earlier travel book, *Maiden*

Voyage, should also be revisted.

Josephine Tey wrote several detective novels during her short life. In *The Daughter of Time*, the novel I read in my hospital bed, her detective, Inspector Grant, finds himself in a hospital bed and passes the time by trying to reconstruct the murder of the princes in the tower, and with the help of his research assistant proves that it was King Henry VII and not King Richard III who was responsible for their deaths. A historical who-done-it, resolved without moving from the hospital bed. No fast-paced action, but suspenseful all the same.

How sad it is that such fine writers have been neglected or forgotten. Time and changing fashions take their toll on the best talents. Only a handful survive.

Sometimes short stories have a better chance of survival, because the good ones get picked-up for inclusions in anthologies, and then get selected again and again. One of my earliest short stories, 'The Eyes Have It', is still turning up in anthologies and school readers, fifty years after it was first written. But once a novel goes out of print, it is hard to revive it. And novels date very quickly. Sometimes too much extraneous matter goes into them, whereas the best short stories stick to the essentials.

When I wrote *The Room on the Roof* I had published only two or three short stories, so what was I, still a pimply and skinny youth, doing, trying to write a novel?

My Two Years in London

In a way it was a mistake, because in writing it I used up all the experience I had of life and was left with nothing for a second novel!

But it had to be written.

That last year in Dehra, before I left for England, was now so ingrained in me, so much a part of my emotional make-up, that it had to be expressed in the way I knew best—the written word. The journal had become a novel, and some, Krishan, Meena and the rest stayed alive for me on the printed page. Though it might never have been published and I couldn't be sure of this during the four years that various drafts shuttled between me and Andre Deutsch's editor, Diana Athill, the thing had been done, the catharsis had completed, and I could think of other people, other loves, and try something different.

My editor, Diana Athill, was then a young woman in her thirties. Many years later she was to become quite a celebrity, the author of several successful autobiographies, which were frank, revealing and beautifully written. But when I knew her she hadn't done any writing (or none that I know of), although she was very busy assessing and introducing the work of many promising young writers, novelists such as Jack Kerouac and V.S. Naipaul. Although she did not (could not) teach me how to write (I stubbornly refused to temper my addiction to semi-commas and certain Indianisms), she made me feel that

I was part of her literary world, giving me gossip about others writers and telling me about the books they were publishing. I visited her at her flat in Regent's Park quite often, and even took her to see an Indian picture, *Aan* (the first to get a commercial release in London) but it was a terrible let-down, a very silly film, the sort of Bombay extravaganza that gave a completely misleading and over-romanticized conception of Indians. I felt more at ease introducing her to paan at a little Indian restaurant near Fitzroy Square, but I'm afraid she didn't care much for paan either. My efforts to make Diana an Indophile were not very successful. But she liked my book. 'I can see why you love India,' she said, 'It's so easy to make friends.'

But my first appearance in print (in London, that is) really came about as a result of my lengthy stay in the Hampstead General Hospital. A fellow patient, an English boy of about my age (perhaps a little younger) turned out to be a good reader, and when he was discharged he gave me a copy of a magazine for teenagers called *Young Elizabethan*. A couple of months later, when I was back at my typewriter, I sent them one of my short stories. It was published, and paid for. And even after I had returned to India I continued to write for the *Elizabethan*, and several of my early stories appeared in it—'The Thief,' 'The Long Day', 'The Big Race,' 'The Stolen Daffodils,' among others—until it closed down around 1959.

My Two Years in London

And while still in that hospital bed, I had written a piece called 'My Two Homes'—about an English boy growing up in an Indian home—and this became a talk that I gave on BBC Radio. The BBC's Home Service also ran a weekly short story programme, and when I returned to India and started freelancing, many of my early stories found a home with them. 'The Night Train at Deoli', 'The Woman on Platform 8', and many others were read by Robert Rietti, a fine actor in radio plays. Back in Dehra, I would drop in on a friend who had a short-wave radio, and listened spellbound to my stories being beamed to me from distant London.

So my two years in London were a good preparation for the years of struggle that lay ahead, when I returned to India. Although my job was a dull one, I did find time to write, to read, to visit the theatre, to wander about the streets of London (getting to know that city fairly well), and so banishing the loneliness that awaited me whenever I returned to cold bed-sitting room.

And there were friends too. Students, mostly, who came in and out of my life at random.

Praven, a Gujarati boy who was a little younger than me; he liked visiting pubs and night clubs! I had no idea what he was studying—I never saw him with a book—but he was the recipient of regular remittances from his father in Bombay.

Thanh, a Vietnamese, who cultivated me because he wanted to 'improve his English', he dropped me when he discovered I spoke English with an Indian accent.

Vu-phuong, also Vietnamese, who used to tell me my fortune with tea-leaves. When you finish drinking your tea, you let the tea-leaves settle naturally, and the pattern they form gives you an indication of what to expect in the future. This was great fun, because it meant sharing innumerable cups of tea with Vu, with whom I fell in love. But when I asked her to marry me, she said it was not in the tea-leaves.

Just as well, perhaps. If I'd been married in England (or Vietnam), I might never have returned to India.

And returning to India was still very much my first priority.

But first I had to save a little money, publish my novel, and try to see a little better with my right eye.

The best way to get to know a city is to walk all over the place. So I walked all over Soho and the West End; I walked from Primrose Hill down to Baker Street, looking for Sherlock Holmes, but couldn't find him; I walked all over the East End, looking for places described by Dickens in *Oliver Twist* and *Our Mutual Friend*, but they looked very different from what I'd imagined; I walked around Kensington Gardens, looking for Peter Pan, but he must have been away in Neverland. So I went to Kew

Gardens, and felt quite at home in a big glass hothouse, surrounded by tropical plants of every description, after that, whenever I felt homesick, I went down to Kew—not just in lilac time, but any time...

Andre Deutsch finally gave me a £50 advance for *The Room on the Roof*. I did not wait for it to be published, but bought a ticket to Bombay for £40; gave a week's notice to my kind employers, who presented me with a travel bag; and boarded the M.S. Batory at Southampton, accompanied by said travel bag and an old suitcase bulging with books and a few clothes. It was March, 1955, and I was twenty-one years old. I had left India to seek my fortune in the West; and now I was returning to the East to find, if not fortune, at least fulfilment of a sort.

Although I was over twenty, and had been earning my own living for over these years, in many ways I was still a boy, with a boy's thoughts and dreams—dreams of romance, high adventure and good companionship. And I was still a lonely boy, alone on that big ship— passengers and crew all strangers to me—sailing into an uncertain future.

I had two books with me—Thoreau's *Walden* and Richard Jefferies' *The Story of My Heart*—both reflecting my burgeoning interest in the natural world—but during the day the cabin was hot and stuffy, and the decks, too crowded, so I postponed most of my reading until the journey was over. But at night, when it was cool on the deck, and most of the passengers were down below, watching a film or drinking Polish vodka (the Batory was a Polish ship), I would sit out under the stars while the ship ploughed on through the Red Sea, bringing me home to India. There was no sound but the dull thunder of the ship's screws and the faint tinkle of music from an open porthole.

And as I sat there, pondering over my future, a line from Thoreau kept running through my head. 'Lonely! Why should I feel lonely? Is not our planet in the Milky Way?'

Wherever I went, the stars were there to keep me company. And I knew that as long as I connected, in both a physical and mystical way, with the natural world—sea, sun, earth, moon and stars—I would never feel lonely upon this planet.

My Limehouse Adventure

So this was Limehouse: quiet, empty back-streets, with the river lapping against the walls of old houses. A brewery. A few warehouses. A boy speeding along the pavement on roller-skates.

But was this the real Limehouse? There were no drunken sailors on the streets. There were no Chinese laundry-houses. Shouldn't a lascar come stumbling out of a dark doorway with a knife in his back? Wasn't it somewhere on this very street that Watson found Holmes in an opium-den run by a heavily-scarred Malay, while stairs above someone screamed and outside there was a splash in the river?

Where were Edgar Wallace's sinister Chinese, and where were the characters of W.W. Jacobs?

Limehouse on a Sunday. Neither Chelsea nor Hampstead could have been more tranquil. Of course the pubs would close soon and then perhaps the West Indian sailors, now sitting quietly in front of the bar, might suddenly come to life and perform calypsos in the street. Neither Mods nor Rockers were anywhere to be seen.

I was feeling hungry, since I had walked almost the entire length of the Commercial Road, starting from Petticoat Lane where I had found myself handling over five shillings to a street photographer for taking any picture unasked. (An hour later, when I looked at the photograph, it had faded completely.)

On Ming Street—a name reminiscent of more exotic times—I was delighted to find several small restaurants with Chinese names. Most of them were empty. There was a time when you could count the Chinese in Limehouse by the thousands, but now there weren't more than two or three hundred in the area.

I pushed my way through the swing doors of the Nanking Restaurant and looked around. The place was empty. Tables and chairs were painted a bright green, and decorating the walls were coloured pictures of George

My Limehouse Adventure

V, George VI and Elizabeth II. I had never seen such a patriotic display anywhere other than in the East End.

There was nobody in the restaurant, not even a waiter, so I sat down and rattled a salt-cellar in order to attract attention. But as no one came, I began to wonder if the owner of the place couldn't afford a waiter and did the serving himself, but even he was nowhere to the seen. The room was as quiet as an empty chapel.

I coughed. The sound startled me. I tried whistling, but it sounded eerie rather than cheerful. I noticed a jug of water standing on a side-board, and feeling thirsty, got up and made for it. As I couldn't find a glass, I drank the water straight from the jug.

I was putting it down when an inner door burst open and an excited Chinese rushed out. Without so much as a glance in my direction, he went through the swing doors and stood uncertainly on the pavement, looking in all directions, before coming in again with an anxious, distracted expression.

Without a word, he returned to the inner room.

Here was a mystery! Limehouse was behaving in a way which was true to its reputation. Perplexed but undaunted, I returned to my table, determined to remain in the restaurant until someone took notice of me.

The sign-board outside proclaimed that the place was a restaurant; and as the doors were open, I had every right to sit at a table, and wait to be served or possibly murdered.

Presently, I heard a curtain rustle. It was a girl who came out—a little Chinese girl of about eleven, with her hair in a pigtail and green woolen leggings on her feet. Like the man, she paid no attention to me, but began bouncing a rubber ball on the floor. It bounced too high and came towards me, so I caught it and placed it on the table.

'Pass the ball,' said the girl from the middle of the room.

'Come and get it,' I said, 'And can I get anything to eat here?'

'If you like. Pass the ball.'

'Was that your father who came out just now?'

'Yes. Aren't you going to pass the ball?'

'Tell me, does he serve his customers, or do they just go into the kitchen and help themselves?'

'You'll have to wait', said the girl. 'My mother's having a baby.'

I threw the ball across the table. She caught it neatly, marched out through the swing-doors, and began bouncing the ball on the pavement. As soon as she had gone, I heard a baby crying in the inner room. For about five minutes I sat listening, and then I began to feel foolish. I was about to leave when the Chinese came bustling into the room, his face creased with smiles.

'I am very sorry, sir!' he exclaimed. 'I have made you wait a long time. But the doctor could not arrive in time, and the baby would not wait for the doctor. So my wife and I—we had to manage by ourselves. All is well now, sir. Here is the menu.'

I gazed at him in wonder, while he bubbled over with enthusiasm.

'Your lunch is on the house, sir,' he said. 'Chicken noodle, chow-mien, lobster fuyong, anything you like! We have had six children, but all girls. Now we have a boy!'

I congratulated him, and accepted the offer of lunch. It was a good meal, lovingly prepared. The long wait had been worthwhile and Limehouse had after all, come up to my expectations. Where else in London could this have happened to me?

Journey to Mathura

Mathura, most sacred of cities, stands on the right bank of the Jamuna, north-west of Agra. All men speak of Mathura with reverence, and it has been said, 'If a man spent in Benares all his lifetime, he has earned less merit than if he passes but a single day in the sacred city of Mathura.'

It is difficult to pierce the fog which hides the date of the city's birth; but sacred it has always been, as the capital of the kingdom of Braj, and the birthplace of Lord Krishna—'Teacher and soul of the Universe, destroyer of the earth's tyrant kings, and the First of the Spirits…'

Journey to Mathura

I went to Mathura at the end of the rains. The fields and the trees were alive with strange, beautiful birds: the long-tailed king-crow; innumerable doves in shades of blue and grey; kingfishers and bluejays and weaver-birds; and, resting on a telegraph pole, the great white-headed kite, which, some say, was Garuda, Vishnu's famous steed. Resplendent, too, were the green and gold parrots, from among whom Kamadeva, the God of love, chose his steed. Armed with his sugarcane bow with its string made of bees, Kamadeva still rides at night over the plains of Mathura. Many of the journeys he makes are on nights approaching the full moon. He knows the ways of men and women, and his bow, like Cupid's, is always ready to assist the ardent lover.

In the tanks and jheels around Mathura I saw a variety of game birds—wild ducks, herons, cranes and snipes—but all life is sacred for many miles around Mathura, and not even the bird-trapper is permitted to lay his snares.

Strutting under an old tamarind tree are Krishna's birds, the brilliant peacocks. Centuries ago, they gave the city their name, and today Mathura is still known as the 'Peacock City'. The peacocks seem to know that they are chosen by Krishna. Spreading out their many-coloured fan-tails, they glance at us drab mortals with an air of superiority.

Near Mathura is Brindaban, in the forests of which—

they are not there anymore—the young Krishna and his brother Balaram ran wild, playing on their shepherd's pipes. The neighbours found Krishna very mischievous. He was extremely fond of butter and, going by stealth one day to the house of a neighbour, climbed on to a shelf to get at a large jar of butter. He ate the butter as far as he could reach, and then got into the jar. The owner, on returning, found him there, and putting a cover on the jar to prevent the boy from escaping, went to Krishna's father to complain. But when he arrived at the house, it was not the father who met him, but the little butter-thief.

There is another story which tells us of the day Krishna stole his mother's curd, and finished eating it while no one was looking. 'Oh, you wicked one!' exclaimed his mother, when she discovered what had happened. 'Come, let me see your mouth.' And when she looked into his mouth, she saw the Universe—the earth, sea and heavens; the sun and the moon, the planets and all the stars...

Brindaban stands on a tongue of land surrounded by the river, which has curved here in a strange fashion. Legends tell us that Balaram, who was very strong, once led a dance on the Jamuna's bank, but moved his giant limbs so clumsily that the river laughed aloud and taunted him, saying: 'Enough, my clumsy child! How can you hope to dance as Krishna, who is divine?' This made

Journey to Mathura

Balaram very angry with the river, and taking his great plough, he traced a furrow from the brink of the river; and so deep was the furrow that the river fell into it, and was led very far astray.

When the tyrant King Kamsa heard of the unusual exploits of Krishna and Balaram, he planned to have them killed in case they became a danger to his power. He sent a message to the brothers, inviting them to a contest of arms in the royal city of Mathura. Krishna and Balaram accepted.

On the day of the contest, King Kamsa sat on a lofty throne near the arena. As Krishna and Balaram entered, a mighty elephant was sent against them. But Krishna, seizing the animal by the tail, swung it around his head and threw it to the ground. Then each of the brothers taking a tusk, slew Kamsa's mightiest champions. Kamsa ordered his army to kill the boys, but Krishna sprang up the steps of the throne, seized the King by his hair, and hurled him into a deep ravine.

Visitors to Mathura are still shown the mound where Kamsa's throne once stood. And still venerated is that part of the river-front where the two boys rested after dragging the body of Kamsa down to the funeral-pyre.

I wandered in the streets of the city, past shops gleaming with brass-work or piled high with pedas, Mathura's famous sweets. From the bridge, we could see the river-face with its innumerable temples. And below, hundreds of majestic tortoises watched the bathers and the boatmen with speculative eyes. Sometimes a bather seized one of these long-necked creatures, and held it up for a better view. The tortoise would immediately draw its legs into its shell, illustrating the belief that nothing is annihilated but only disappears, the effect being absorbed in the cause.

The Taj at High Noon

It is high noon on a summer's day in Agra, and I am the only visitor at the Taj.

'You should see the Taj by moonlight,' everyone tells me; but these are dark nights, and anyway, I have to be in Delhi in a few hours. Instead of lingering and loafing as I am usually given to doing, I find myself chained, like a package-tour tourist, to a time-schedule. I have only one hour to spend at the magnificent mausoleum built by an Emperor to preserve the memory of a cherished wife. And so, like mad dogs and Englishman, I go out in the mid-day sun.

It is difficult to view the Taj at high noon. The fierce sun strikes the white marble, and there is a great dazzle of reflected light. One stands there with averted eyes, looking at everything—the formal gardens, the surrounding walls of red sandstone, the scene across the river—everything except the monument one has come to see.

It is there, of course, very solid and real, perfectly preserved, with every jade, jasper or lapis-lazuli stone embedded in its rightful place; and after a while one can shade one's eyes and take in a vision of shimmering white marble. The heat rises in waves from the pavement, and the squares of black and white marble create an effect of running water. Inside the chamber it is cool and dark and, after a while, rather musty—so much so that one hurries up again into the blazing sunlight.

I walk the length of a gallery and turn with some relief to the river scene. The sluggish Jamuna winds past Agra on its way to union with the Ganga. I know the Jamuna well. I know where it emerges from the foothills, cold and blue from the melting snows; I know it as it winds through fields of wheat and mustard and sugar-cane, across the flat plains of Uttar Pradesh sometimes placid, sometimes in flood. I know the river at Delhi, where its muddy banks are a patchwork of clothes spread out by the hundreds of washermen who serve the city.

And I know it at Mathura, where it is alive with

huge turtles. Mathura, sacred city, whose beginnings are lost in antiquity; birthplace of Lord Krishna, whose every exploit is linked with the riverside ghats, forests and temples. And then the river wends its way through Agra, to this spot by the Taj, where parrots flash in the sunshine, and kingfishers swoop low over the water, and a proud peacock struts across the grass that carpets the approach to the monument.

I followed the peacock into a shady grove. It is quite tame and does not fly away. It leads me to a small boy who is sitting in the shade of a tree feasting on a handful of some small green fruit.

I have not seen this fruit before; I ask the boy what it is. He offers me what looks like a hard green plum.

'It is called Kamrak,' says the boy. 'There are many Kamrak trees in the garden.'

'Are you allowed to pick the fruit?' I ask.

'I am allowed,' he says, flashing me a smile. 'My father is the head gardener!'

I bite into the fruit. It is hard and sour, but not unpleasant.

'Do you live here?' I ask.

'On the other side of the wall,' he says. 'But I come here every day, to help my father—and to eat the fruit.'

'So you see the Taj Mahal every day?'

'I have seen it every day for as long as I can remember.'

Journey Down the Years

'And I am seeing it today only... You are very lucky!'

He shrugs. 'If you see it once, or a hundred times, it is the same thing. It doesn't change.'

'Don't you like looking at the Taj?'

'I like looking at the people who come here. They are always different. In the evenings, when it is cool, there are many people.'

'You must have seen people from almost every country in the world.'

'That is true. They all come here to look at the Taj. And I look at them. In that way, it isn't boring.'

'Well, you have the Taj to thank for that.'

He looks thoughtfully at the shimmering monument. His eyes are accustomed to the fierce sun; but it seems as though he is looking at the Taj for the first time. He sees it every day but at this moment he is really looking at it. He is thinking about it, wondering what magic it must possess to attract people from all corners of the earth, to bring them here walking through his father's well-kept garden so that he can have something new and fresh to look at each day.

And as he looks, a cloud—a very small cloud—passes across the face of the sun; and in the softened light I am able to look at the Taj without screwing up my eyes and I see it in all its splendour.

As the boy said, it doesn't change. Therein lies its

beauty. For the effect on the traveller is the same today as it was three hundred years ago when the Frenchman, Bernier, wrote: 'Nothing offends the eye....... No part can be found that is not skillfully wrought, or that has not its peculiar beauty.'

And so, for a few moments, this poem in marble is on view for two people—the traveller and the gardener's boy.

We say nothing; there is nothing to be said.

But now, many months later, when I try to recapture the essence of that day, it is not the monument itself that I remember most vividly. The Taj is there, of course: I still see it as a mirror for the sun. But what remains with me more than anything else is the passage of the river and the sharp flavour of the Kamrak fruit.

The Gallery of Birds

Having divided the last ten years of my life between Delhi and Mussoorie, I have come to the heretical conclusion that there is more bird life in cities than there in the hills and forests around our hill-stations. For birds to survive, they have to learn to live with and upon humans and those birds like crows, sparrows and mynahs who do this to perfection, continue to thrive as our cities grow, whereas the purely wild birds, those who depend upon the forests for life, are rapidly disappearing, simply because the forests are disappearing.

Recently, I saw more birds in one week in a New Delhi

The Gallery of Birds

colony than I had seen during a month in the hills. In the hills, one must be patient and alert if one is to spot just a few of the birds so beautifully described in Salim Ali's *Indian Hill Birds*. The babblers and thrushes are still around but the fly-catchers and warblers are seldom seen or heard.

But in Delhi, if you have just a bit of garden and perhaps a guava tree, you will be visited by innumerable bulbuls, tailor birds mynahs, hoopoes, parrots and treepies. Or if you own an old house you will have to share it with pigeons and sparrows, perhaps swallows or swifts. And if you have neither a garden nor a rooftop, you will be visited by crows.

Wherever man goes, the crow follows. He has learnt to perfect the art of living off humans. He will, I am sure, be the first bird on the moon, scavenging among the paper bags and cartons left behind by untidy astronauts.

Crows favour the densest areas of human population and there must be at least one for every human. Many crows have obviously been humans in previous lives; they are as cunning and possess the sense of self-preservation of the human being. At the same time, there are many humans who have obviously been crows and haven't lost their thieving instincts.

Watch a crow sidling along a garden wall with a shabby genteel air, cocking a speculative eye at the kitchen door and any attendant humans. He reminds me of a newspaper reporter hovering in the background until his chance comes—then pouncing! I have even known a crow to make off with an egg from the breakfast table. No other bird except perhaps the sparrow has been so successful in exploiting human beings.

The mynah, although he too is quite at home in the city, is more of a gentleman. He prefers fruit on the tree to scraps from the kitchen, and visits the garden much out of a sense of sociability as in expectation of hand-outs. He is quite handsome too, with his bright orange bill and the mask around his eyes. He is equally at home on a railway platform as on the ear of a grazing buffalo, and, being omnivorous, has no trouble in co-existing with man.

The sparrow on the other hand is not a gentleman. Uninvited, he enters your home, followed by his friends, relatives and political hangers-on, and proceeds to quarrel and leave his droppings on the sofa cushions with a complete disregard for the presence of humans. The party will then proceed towards the garden and destroy all the flower buds. No birds have succeeded so well in making fools out of humans.

Although the bluejay (or roller) is quite capable of making his living in the forest, he seems to show a preference for the haunts of men and would rather perch on a telegraph wire than in a tree. Probably, he finds the

The Gallery of Birds

wire a better launching pad for his sudden rocket flights and aerial acrobatics. In repose, he is rather shabby but in flight when his outspread wings reveal his brilliant blues, he takes one's breath away. His food consists of beetles and other insects and pests, he can be considered a friend and an ally.

Parrots make little or no distinction between town and country life. They are the freelancers of the bird world—sturdy, independent and noisy. With flashes of blue and green, they swoop across the road, settle for a while in a mango tree and then with shrill, delighted cries, move on to some other field or orchard. They will sample all the food they can without finishing any. They are destructive birds but because of their bright plumage, graceful flight and charming ways, are popular favourites and can get away with anything. No one who has enjoyed watching a flock of parrots in carefree flight would want to cage one of these virile birds. Yet many people do cage them.

After the peacock, perhaps the most popular bird in rural India is the sarus crane—a familiar sight around jheels and river banks of northern India and Gujarat. The sarus pairs for life and is seldom seen without its mate. When one bird dies, the other often pines away and seemingly dies of grief. It is this near human quality of devotion that has earned the birds this popularity with the villagers of the plains. As a result they are well-protected.

In the long run, it is the 'common man' and not the scientist or conservationist who can best give protection to the birds and animals living around him. Religious sentiment has helped preserve the peacock and a few other birds. It is a pity that other equally beautiful birds do not enjoy the same protection.

But the wily crow, the cheeky sparrow and the sensible mynah will always be with us. Quite possibly they will survive even longer than the human species. And it is the same with other animals. While the cringing jackal has learnt the art of survival, his master, the magnificent tiger is on its way to extinction.

The Charming Bloodsucker

No, this article is not about the village moneylender, but about the garden lizard—a little creature who is found in almost every Indian garden and who has done nothing to deserve the name by which he is known.

How this lizard came by the name of bloodsucker is a mystery, because it certainly does not suck blood. This misnomer might have originated through a popular superstition in some parts of the India. There are people who believe that this harmless lizard—its real name is Calotes versicolor—has the power of sucking a person's blood simply by looking at him. It is also believed that the lizard changes its colour to red because of the blood it has absorbed in this way!

Not Conspicous

Give a lizard a bad name and it's sure to stick. And so the harmless garden lizard, like the equally harmless gecko or wall lizard, has been credited with all the powers of darkness and is often cruelly put to death.

The bloodsucker (too late to change its name to anything else) does of course change its colour to some degree under ordinary circumstances, although it is not as gifted as the chameleon in this respect; it reserves its most vivid colour changes for the breeding season. So if you see a garden lizard turning a bright red, this is not because it is absorbing your blood, but because it is in love—not with you, but with a female of its own species.

As a rule the bloodsucker is not conspicuous. This is not because it remains in hiding. It likes warmth and light, and may often be seen basking in the morning sun, on the alert for some unwary insect. Light brown or greyish, its colour easily blends with the varied hues of its surroundings, which is why it often goes unnoticed.

During the cold season, bloodsuckers seek shelter in hollow trunks or holes in the ground, or enter houses where they hide behind furniture and curtains. They emerge from these retreats only during the warmest time of the day, to sunbathe and indulge in a little exercise. During the summer months they spend nearly all their time in the open.

It is during the breeding season that they undergo a remarkable change of colour. While the female confines herself to a maidenly blush, the male dons the most gaudy attire, his head, shoulders and a part of his forelegs becoming crimson or scarlet, while black patches appear on either side of the throat and on the shoulders.

The gorgeously painted male sits on a fence or the trunk of a tree, surveying the neighbourhood. His manners are as loud as his dress, and he is out to seek a quarrel. From time to time he will jerk his head and shoulders up and down, a challenge to all other males in the vicinity.

Like Warriors

Two males about to fight will first charge each other from a distance like warriors of old. On meeting, both stand on hind legs and fall, gripping each other with forelegs and trying to bite. Toes or a portion of the tail often get bitten off in such an encounter. However, even with lizards—as with professional wrestlers—there is a good deal of pretence and very often the fight stops as abruptly as it began, one of the lizards making a hasty retreat.

At the time of courtship a curious performance is put through by the male. He chooses a convenient spot, then advances cautiously towards the female. He is then a pale flesh-colour. He stands upright raising the forepart of the body as high as possible and solemnly nods his head up and down. As he does this, his mouth rapidly opens and closes a number of times. Then, as he closes upon the female, his colours grow more vivid. But after separating he is almost colourless again.

If the amorous male is driven away, caught, or killed, the dark spot disappears entirely from his neck; and as happens among almost all forms of life, another male takes his place within a few hours.

Apart from superstitious humans, the garden lizard's chief enemies are large birds such as crows or bluejays who are only too ready to make a meal of him. But the bloodsucker is an agile little creature and his long slender tail, which easily comes apart from the rest of his body, is also a great protection. It often happens that a bird seizes a lizard by the long tail. Then the lizard, by leaving its tail behind in the bird's beak, is able to escape with its life. The bird goes on killing the old tail, and the lizard begins growing a new one.

Gentle Shade by Day

Those who have spent time in non-air-conditioned parts of India will remember with gratitude those gracious trees that provide shade and shelter during the summer months—the banyan, peepul, mango, neem and others. Coastal dwellers are not so fortunate for there is not much shade to be had from a palm tree unless you keep moving in its long but insubstantial shadow.

I am not surprised that the sages of old were given to sitting beneath the peepul tree. They might have had various religious reasons for calling it sacred but I am sure there was a good practical reason as well. Few trees provide a cooler shade than it does. Even on the stillest of days, the peepul leaves are forever twirling and with thousands of leaves spinning like tops, there is quite a breeze for anyone sitting below.

However, there are warnings about peepul trees— 'Gentle shade by day and terror by night!' During the night the tree is said to be alive with various spirits, most of them inimical to man. One is advised not to sleep beneath it for this is construed by a ghost as an invitation to jump down your throat and take possession of you, or at the very least ruin your digestion.

It is also said to be unlucky to sleep beneath a tamarind, but I have often reclined in the pleasant shade of this noble tree and have come to no harm. A famous tamarind stands over the tomb of Tansen, the great musician and singer of Akbar's court at Gwalior. Its leaves, though bitter, are eaten by singers to improve their voices.

A mango grove is a wonderful place for an afternoon siesta. But if the mangoes are ripening, there is usually a great deal of activity going on with parrots, crows, monkeys and small boys, all attempting to evade the watchman who uses an empty kerosene tin as a drum to try and frighten them away. So it's not the ideal place for a nap then, but the shade under a mango grove is dark, deep and very soothing.

Gentle Shade by Day

The banyan tree with its aerial roots represents the matted hair of Lord Shiva. There is always shade and space beneath a venerable old banyan. It is still a popular community centre in our Indian villages but is becoming a rarity in cities simply because it covers so large an area. And if you cut its aerial roots the tree topples over. Other handsome trees related to the banyan are the pilkhan and the chilkhan, large spreading evergreens, both quite noticeable on some of New Delhi's wider avenues.

The neem is a tall tree, but its numerous branches give it a shady head. One of my greatest pleasures is to walk beneath an avenue of neem trees after a shower of rain. As the fallen berries are crushed underfoot they give out a sharp heady fragrance, which I find exhilarating. Apart from its medicinal uses, the tree is connected in legends with the Sun God as in the story of *Neembarak*. 'The Sun in a Neem Tree' who invited to dinner a Bairagi tribal whose rules forbade him to eat anything except by daylight. When dinner was delayed after sundown, Suraj Narayan, the Sun God, obligingly descended from a neem tree and continued shining till dinner was over.

On this pleasant note I end this tribute, only adding that shade-giving trees symbolize the harmony between man and nature and that our ancestors in their devotion to trees and reverence for them, clearly showed that they knew what was good for them.

Gran's Kitchen

As kitchens went, it wasn't very big. What made it fabulous was all that came out of it. Gran's curries and kebabs, chocolate fudge and peanut toffee, jellies and gulab jamuns, meat pies and apple pies, stuffed chickens, stuffed eggplants, and even ham, stuffed with stuffed chicken! As far as I was concerned, Gran was the best cook in the world.

The town we lived in was called Dehradun. It's still there, though much bigger and more populous since India's independence. Gran had a large, rambling bungalow on the outskirts of town. On the grounds were many fruit

Gran's Kitchen

trees—mangoes, lichees, guavas, bananas, papayas and lemons—there was room for all of them, including a giant jackfruit tree that threw its shadow on the walls of the house.

Gran had a saying,

'Blessed is the house upon whose walls

The shade of an old tree softly falls.'

She was right, hers was a good house to live in, especially for a ten-year-old boy with a tremendous appetite.

Every winter, when I came home from boarding school, I would spend at least a month with Gran before going over to my parents in Assam. My father managed a tea plantation there, and although the tea gardens were fun to play in, my parents couldn't cook. Like most colonials, they employed a Khansama, a professional cook, who made good mutton curry but little else. So I was always glad to spend half my holidays with Gran.

Gran was glad to have me too, because she lived alone most of the time. Not entirely alone, though. The gardener, his son Mohan and a mongrel dog named Crazy all lived in the compound. And sometimes there was Uncle Ken, a nephew of Gran's, who came to stay whenever he was out of a job (which was fairly often), or when he felt like enjoying some of Gran's cooking.

Gran didn't enjoy cooking just for herself; she liked

to have someone to cook for. And although Uncle Ken sometimes appreciated her efforts, and Crazy loved her table scraps, a good cook likes a kid to feed, because kids are adventurous and ready to try even the most unusual dishes.

Whenever Gran tried out a new recipe on me, she would wait for my reaction, and then jot down some of my comments in a notebook. This was useful when she wanted to try the same dish on others.

'Do you like it?' she'd ask, after I'd taken a few mouthfuls.

'Yes, Gran.'

'Sweet enough?'

'Yes, Gran.'

'Not *too* sweet?'

'No, Gran.'

'Would you like some more?'

'Yes please, Gran.'

'Well, finish it off.'

'Mmmm...'

'Eat well, but don't overeat,' Gran used to tell me. And we did eat well, even though all those wonderful meals consisted of only one course followed by a sweet dish. It was Gran's cooking that turned a modest meal into a feast.

Roast duck was one of her specialties. The first time I

had roast duck at Gran's place, Uncle Ken was there too. He'd just lost his job as a railway guard, and had come to stay with Gran until he could find something else.

Uncle Ken ate just as much as I did, but he never praised Gran's dishes and that annoyed me. He looked at the roast duck, his glasses slipping down to the edge of his nose. 'Hmmm... Duck again, Aunt May?'

'What do you mean by duck *again*? We haven't had duck since you were here last month!'

'That's what I mean,' said Uncle Ken. 'Somehow, one expects a little more variety.'

All the same, he took two large helpings and ate most of the stuffing before I could get at it. I got my revenge by emptying all the applesauce onto my plate. Uncle Ken knew I loved stuffing, and I knew he was crazy about Gran's applesauce. So we were even.

Gran was famous all over Dehra for her pickles. Green mangoes, pickled in oil, were always popular. So was her hot lime pickle. And she was adept at pickling turnips, carrots, cauliflowers, and chillies. She could pickle almost any fruit or vegetable—everything from nasturtium seeds to jackfruit.

One winter, when Gran's funds were low, Mohan and I went from house to house...selling pickles for her. Major Clarke, our neighbour across the road, was our first customer.

'And what have you got there?' he asked.

'Pickles, sir.'

'Pickles? Did you make them?'

'No, sir, they're my grandmother's. We're selling them so we can buy a turkey for Christmas.'

'Mrs Bond's pickles, eh? Well, I'm glad this is the first house on your route, because that basket will soon be empty. There's no one who can make a pickle like your grandmother! What have you this time? Stuffed chillies, I hope. She knows they're my favorite. I shall be deeply wounded if there are no stuffed chillies in that basket.'

There were, in fact, three bottles of stuffed red chillies in the basket, and Major Clarke bought all of them.

Further down the road, Dr Dutt bought several bottles of lime pickle, saying it was good for his liver. And Mr Hari, who owned a garage at the end of the road, purchased two bottles of pickled onions and begged us to bring another as soon as we could.

By the time we got home, the basket was empty, and Gran was richer by thirty rupees—enough, in those days, for a turkey.

Uncle Ken stayed for Christmas and ate most of the turkey.

A Book Lover's Life-Long Hunt

My mother and stepfather were not great readers, and books were a scarce commodity in my life until I was about twelve. In those lonely childhood years, I was to discover that books could be good friends, steadfast and reliable, and I seized upon almost any printed matter that came my way, whether it was a girls' classic like *Little Women*, or a *True Detective* magazine, or Edgar Allan Poe, or 'Insect Life in Mozambique'.

Fifty years on, my reading habits are still as wide-ranging and omnivorous.

But I think it all began in that forest rest house in

the Siwalik Hills, a subtropical range cradling the Doon Valley in northern India. Here my stepfather and gun-toting friends were given to hunting the wild animals that still roamed those forests. He was a poor shot, so he cannot really be blamed for the absence of wildlife today; but he did his best to shoot down everything in sight!

On one of these 'shikar' trips, we were staying in a rest house near the Timli Pass. My stepfather and his friends were 'after the tiger', and set out every morning with an army of villagers to 'beat' the jungle, in order to drive the tiger out into the open. Never excited by this form of sport, I stayed behind in the rest house, fully expecting complete boredom for the duration of our stay. Exploring the old rest house, I discovered that one of the rooms was furnished with a dusty bookshelf, stacked high with books that hadn't been touched for years.

It was here that I discovered *Three Men in a Boat*, by Jerome K. Jerome, which I finished reading that same day. The next day I read most of the stories in M.R. James', *Ghost Stories of an Antiquary*. On the third day, while the sportsmen were still looking for their tiger, I chuckled over my first Wodehouse (*Love Among the Chickens*), sampled O. Henry, and began *David Copperfield*. Camp broke up before I could get through *Copperfield*, but the forest ranger said I could keep it, which I did, thus becoming the only person with a trophy to show for the hunt, the clever tiger having proved elusive.

After that adventure, I was always looking for books in unlikely places; and I had a knack of finding them, too.

A couple of years ago, I was rummaging through some discarded books at a school jumble sale, when I found a first edition of *Three Men in a Boat*. As this book had been one of my first loves, I felt that my reading adventures had come full cycle. When I think of all the great books I have read over the years, I realize that they have more than made up for the disappointments that sometimes came my way, and that I am indeed a fortunate man. I am sure that other compulsive readers feel the same way.

Although I never went to college, I think I have read as much, if not more, than most college men, so that it would be true to say that I received my education in second-hand bookshops. London had many, and Calcutta once had a number of them, but I think the prize must go to a small town in Wales called Hay-on-Wye, which has twenty-six bookshops and over one million books. It's in the world's quieter corners that book lovers still flourish as a race.

Unlikely, out-of-the-way places often yield up treasures—like the trunkful thrown out of a hotel storeroom, providing me with *The Complete Plays of J.M. Barrie*. Am I the only person around who still reads Barrie? His occasional sentimentality is a sin in the eyes of modern critics, but I must confess to an unabashed enjoyment of plays such as *Mary Rose, Dear Brutus, A Kiss For Cinderella*, and, of course, *Peter Pan*.

I love discovering forgotten or neglected gems, which I feel deserve to be read again. One of them was an exquisite essay by the Boston writer, Louise Imogen Guiney (1861–1920), called 'The Precept of Peace', which appeared in her book *Patrins* (1897). A lovely and profound piece of writing, it is typical of the humorous tranquillity with which she faced the failure (financially speaking) of all her books.

Another gem, *Sweet Rocket* (1920) by Mary Johnston, was also a financial failure. It had only the thinnest outline of a story, but she set out her ideas in lyrical prose that seduces the sympathetic reader at every turn of the page. Miss Johnston was from Virginia. She did not travel outside America. But her little book did. I found it buried under a pile of railway timetables at a railway bookstall in Simla, the old summer capital of India—almost as though it had been waiting there for me, these seventy years!

Those Fragrant Moments

I would be the last person to belittle a flower for its colour or appearance, but it does happen that my favourites are those with their own distinctive fragrance.

The rose, of course, is a joy to all—even to my baby granddaughter who likes to take it apart, petal by petal; but there are other, less spectacular blooms, which have a lovely and sometimes elusive fragrance all their own.

I have a special fondness for antirrhinums, or snapdragons as they are more commonly known. If I sniff hard at them, I don't seem to catch any scent at all. They seem to hold it back from me. But if I walk past a bed of snapdragons, or even a single plant, the gentlest of sweet fragrances is wafted to me, zephyr-like. And if I stop to try and take it all in, it has gone again! I find this quite tantalizing, but it has given me a special regard for this modest flower.

Carnations, with this scent of cloves, are great show-offs. And here, in India, the jasmine can be rather heady and overpowering. The honeysuckle too has to make its presence known. There is a honeysuckle creeper outside my study-window, and all through the summer its sweet (rather cloying) fragrance drifts in through the open window. This is lovely; but sometimes I have to close it just so that I can give my attention to other less intrusive smells—like the soft scent of petunias (another favourite) and pine-needles on the hillside and great bunches of sweet-peas on the table.

Some flowers can be quite tricky. One would think that the calendula had no scent at all. Certainly the flower gives nothing away. But run your fingers gently over the leaves and then bring them to your face, and you will get the most delicate and pleasant of aromas.

Leaves can often outdo their blooms. The lemon-geranium, for instance, is valued more for its fragrant leaves than for its rather indeterminate flowers. It is the same with verbena. And I cannot recall what ordinary mint looks like in flower. The refreshing aroma of its leaves makes up for an absence of floral display.

The wood and bark of trees are often characterized by a memorable fragrance. Sandalwood is at one extreme. It is pleasant at first, but then it overpowers the senses; and if you rub the wood the scent it emits is even stronger. Eucalyptus, for all its usefulness, is too volatile for me. I favour the root of the liquorice (mulethi) plant. In the West, it has been put to commercial use by confectioners and others, but here in India many people just chew on the wood to clear the throat and sweeten the breath.

Not all plants are fragrant. Some like the asafetida (hing) will keep strong men at bay. Of course, one man's fragrance may well be another creature's unpleasant odour. Geraniums, my Grandmother said, kept snakes away because they couldn't stand the smell of these flowers. She surrounded the bungalow with pots of geraniums. It's true; we never found a snake in the house, so she may have been right!

But snakes must like some smells, close to the ground. When I lie on summer grass in the Himalayas, I am conscious of the many good smells around me—the grass itself, redolent of the morning's dew; bruised clover; wild violets; tiny buttercups and golden stars and strawberry flowers and, oh, so many that I shall never know the names of...

And the earth itself. It smells differently in different

places. But its loveliest fragrance is known only when it receives a shower of rain. And then the scent of the wet earth rises as though it would give something beautiful back to the clouds—a blend of all the fragrant things that grew in it.

Wayside Stations and Platforms

'Romance brought up the nine-fifteen,' wrote Rudyard Kipling, who was among the first to see the tremendous tourist potential of the Indian Railways, and whose first stories were published in Wheeler's Indian Railway Library.

Anyone who has read his novel *Kim* (1901) will not forget the description of the long train journey undertaken by Kim and the Lama which took them from Lahore to Benaras.

'...as the 3.25 a.m. south bound roared in, the sleepers sprang to life, and the station filled with clamour and shoutings, cries of water and sweetmeat vendors, shouts of policemen, and shrill yells of women gathering up their baskets, their families, and their husbands.'

The scene on a busy railway platform is much the same today, only more intensified: the travelling population has increased a hundred-fold, and so has the number of trains. There are now over 7,500 trains operating in a single day—far exceeding the daily volume of traffic in any other country of the world.

In just one day these trains cover over 62,000 kilometres—a far cry from that historic occasion on 16 April 1853, when India's first railway train steamed off in an atmosphere of great excitement from Bori Bunder in Bombay to Thana, just 34 miles away. Crowds cheered, 21 guns boomed a salute, and the band played rousing tunes as the train's 14 carriages carrying 400 special guests chugged slowly into the distance.

Fifty years later, soon after *Kim* was written, India was already criss-crossed by an extensive network of railway lines, bringing north to south and east to west, enabling the majority of Indians to discover the length, breadth and diversity of their country for the first time. Then, as now, we love to travel, especially by train, and every station, large or small, will provide a wonderful cross-section of people: South Indians on their way to the great pilgrim centres of the north; North Indians

Wayside Stations and Platforms

travelling to the beautiful temples of the south; marriage parties thronging the platforms; soldiers going home on leave or returning to their regiments; gurus surrounded by throngs of disciples and followers; VIPs smothered in garlands.

I must confess to a personal weakness for railway platforms. Sometimes I buy a platform ticket just so that I can spend hours on a bench watching trains come and go, passengers arriving and departing, vendors plying their trade, luggage and goods of every description being moved mysteriously to different destinations. Guards blow their whistles, porters argue with passengers, and station masters lose their tempers. I am in empathy with stations and station masters. My maternal grandfather was a station master on the old B.B. and C.I. Railway (Bombay, Baroda and Central Indian Railway), and perhaps that has something to do with it. There is still some engine soot in my blood.

As a short story writer, I have often found that railway station and platforms give me some of my best stories. As there are now over 7,000 railway stations—in effect, 7,000 destinations—in India, I cannot complain of shortage of material. I have only to visit a railway station in order to experience first-hand that seething tide of life that is uniquely Indian. Mark Twain called it the 'perennially ravishing show of Indian railway stations'. There is nothing like it anywhere else in the world. We are not a melting pot of races and religions; we are a mosaic of all these things. A mosaic that is best observed from the trains that pull the glittering pieces together.

The Kangra Valley Railway is one of my own favourite journeys. This particular railway is visible proof that the railway construction engineer can create a work which is in complete harmony with the beauty of the surroundings. Without interfering in any way with the grandeur of mountain and valley, the railway engineers on this line have revealed to the traveller a land of great enchantment. The graceful curves of the rails, the neatness of the culverts, the symmetrical design of the bridges, the directness of the cuttings—all these help to throw into bold relief the ruggedness of the huge crags through which the line plays hide and seek.

By contrast, if you take the train to Simla, you will spend half your time burrowing through the bowels of the earth with the scenic grandeur of the Himalayas blotted out from your vision and the hillsides made to resemble rabbit-warrens.

Instead of boring his way through the mountains, the railway engineer in Kangra skillfully avoided running headlong into the hillside. Instead of following dizzy curves, he cleverly chose to avoid the awkward corners. He must have been a Taoist at heart, taking Nature's way rather than opposing it.

Not that I am averse to travelling by other mountain railways. Throughout my schooldays in Simla, I was propelled up and down the mountain through those 103 soot-filled tunnels. When I grew up and had the choice, I took the rail-car, which was cleaner, swifter and more comfortable. On the way up, it stopped at Barog, where an excellent breakfast was served. I believe the Barog breakfasts are as good as ever. And in December, on the way down, we would buy bunches of mistletoe at the station, for Barog was famous for its mistletoe. Those wayside stations always charmed me—Barog, Dharampur, Kandaghat, Tara Devi.

Mountains in My Blood

It was while I was living in England, in the jostle and drizzle of London, that I remembered the Himalayas at their most vivid. I had grown up amongst those great blue and brown mountains; they had nourished my blood; and though I was separated from them by thousands of miles of ocean, plains and desert, I could not rid them from my system. It is always the same with mountains. Once you have lived with them for any length of time, you belong to them.

And so, in London in March, the fog became a mountain mist, and the boom of traffic became the boom of the Ganges emerging from the foothills.

I remembered a little mountain path which led my restless feet into a cool, sweet forest of oak and rhododendron, and then on to the windswept crest of a naked hilltop. The hill was called Clouds End. It commanded a view of the plains on one side, and of the snow peaks on the other. Little silver rivers twisted across the valley below, where the rice-fields formed a patchwork of emerald green. And on the hill itself, the wind made a hoo-hoo-hoo in the branches of the tall deodars where it found itself trapped. During the rains, cloud enveloped the valley but left the hill alone, an island in the sky.

On a spur of the hill stood the ruins of an old brewery. The roof had long since disappeared, and the rain had beaten the stone floors smooth and yellow. Some enterprising Englishman had spent a lifetime here, making beer for his thirsty compatriots in the plains. Now, moss and ferns and maidenhair grew from the walls. In a hollow beneath a flight of worn stone steps, a wild cat had made its home. It was a beautiful grey creature, black-striped, with pale green eyes. Sometimes it watched me from the steps or the wall, but it never came near.

No one lived on the hill, except occasionally a coal-burner in a temporary grass-thatched hut. But villagers used the path, grazing their sheep and cattle on the grassy slopes. Each cow or sheep had a bell suspended from its neck, to let the shepherd boy know of its whereabouts. The boy could then lie in the sun and eat wild strawberries without fear of losing his animals.

I remembered some of the shepherd boys and girls. There was a boy who played a flute. Its rough, sweet and straightforward notes travelled clearly across the mountain air. He would greet me with a nod of his head, without taking the flute from his lips. There was a girl who was nearly always cutting grass for fodder. She wore heavy bangles on her feet, and long silver earrings. She did not speak much either, but she always had a wide grin on her face when she met me on the path. She used to sing to herself, or to the sheep, to the grass, or to the sickle in her hand. These things I remembered—these, and the smell of pine needles, the silver of oak leaves and the red of maple, the call of the Himalayan cuckoo, and the mist, like a wet face-cloth, pressing against the hills. Odd, how some little incident, some snatch of conversation, comes back to one again and again, in the most unlikely places. Standing in the aisle of a crowded tube train on a Monday morning, my nose tucked into the back page of someone else's newspaper, I suddenly had a vision of a bear making off with a ripe pumpkin.

A bear and a pumpkin—and there, between Goodge Street and Tottenham Court Road stations, all the smells and sounds of the Himalayas came rushing back to me.

The Last Walnut

It was nice to have a walnut tree just outside the window. It was a tree for all seasons. In winter, the branches were bare; but they were smooth, straight and round like the arms of an apsara. In spring, each branch produced a hard bright spear of new leaf. By midsummer the entire tree was in leaf, and towards the end of the monsoon the walnuts, encased in their green jackets, had reached their full maturity.

Then the jackets began to split, revealing the hard brown shell of the walnuts. Inside the shell was the nut itself. Look closely at the nut, and you will notice that it is shaped rather like the human brain. No wonder the ancients prescribed walnuts for headaches.

Every year the tree made us a gift of a basket of walnuts. But last year the walnuts were disappearing one by one, and I was at a loss to know who had been taking them.

Could it have been Bijju, the milkman's son? He was an inveterate tree-climber. But he was usually found up oak trees, gathering fodder for his cows. He told me that the cows did not care for walnuts. He admitted that they had relished my dahlias which they had eaten the previous week, but he denied having given them any walnuts.

Later, I found a fat langur sitting in the walnut tree. I watched him for some time to see if he was going to help himself to the nuts, but he was only sunning himself. When he thought I wasn't looking, he came down and ate the geraniums; but he did not take any walnuts.

It wasn't the woodpecker. He was out there every day, knocking furiously against the bark of the tree, trying to prise an insect out of a narrow crack. He was strictly non-vegetarian and none the worse for it.

The walnuts had been disappearing early in the morning, while I was still in bed. So one morning I surprised everyone, including myself, by getting up before sunrise. I was just in time to catch the culprit climbing down the walnut tree.

The Last Walnut

She was an old woman, who sometimes came to cut grass on the hillside. Her face was as wrinkled as the walnuts she had been pinching. But in spite of her age, her arms and legs were sturdy. When she saw me, she was as swift as a civet-cat in getting out of the tree.

'Only two,' she said with a giggle, offering them to me on her outstretched palm.

I took one of the walnuts; and thus encouraged, she climbed back into the tree and helped herself to the remaining walnuts. It was impossible to object. I was taken up in admiring her agility in the tree, and wondering if I could ever do the same.

Last winter the PWD decided to take a new road past my doorstep, and the first casualty was the walnut tree. Along with a large number of different trees growing below the cottage, it fell to the contractors' axes.

Recently when I met the old woman on the road, I asked her, 'Where do you get your walnuts now, Grandmother?'

'Nowhere,' she answered stoically. 'That was the last walnut tree on the hillside.'

The Vanishing Trees

The peace and quiet of the Maplewood hillside disappeared forever one winter. The powers that be decided to build another new road into the mountains and the PWD saw fit to take it right past the cottage, about six feet from the window which overlooked the forest.

In my journal, I wrote: Already they have felled most of the trees. The walnut was one of the first to go. A tree I had lived with for over ten years, watching it grow as I had watched Prem's young son Rakesh grow up, looking forward to its new leaf-buds, the broad green leaves of summer turning to spears of gold in September when

The Vanishing Trees

the walnuts were ripe and ready to fall. I knew this tree better than the others. It was just below the window where a buttress for the road is going up.

Another tree I will miss is the young deodar, the only one growing in this stretch of the woods. Some years ago it was stunted due to lack of sunlight. The oaks covered it with their shaggy branches, so I cut away some of the overhanging ones and after that the deodar grew much faster. It was just coming into its own this year—now cut down in its prime, like my young brother on the road to Delhi last month. Both victims of the road—the tree killed by the PWD, my brother by a truck.

Twenty oaks have been felled just in this small stretch near the cottage. By the time this bypass reaches Jabarkhet, about six miles from here, over a thousand oaks will have been slaughtered, besides many other fine trees—maples, deodars and pines—most of them unnecessary as they grew some 50 or 60 yards from the roadside.

The trouble is, hardly anyone (with the exception of the contractor who buys the felled trees) really believes that trees and shrubs are necessary. They get in the way so much, don't they? According to my milkman, the only useful tree is the one which can be picked clean of its leaves for fodder! Another young man remarked to me, 'You should come to Pauri. The view is terrific, there's not a tree on the way!'

Well, he can stay here now and enjoy the ravaged hillside. But as the oaks have gone, the milkman will have to look further afield for his fodder.

Rakesh calls the maples 'butterfly trees' because when the winged seeds fall, they flutter like butterflies in the breeze. No maples now. No bright red leaves to flame against the sky. No birds! That is to say, no birds near the house. No longer will it be possible for me to open the window and watch the scarlet minivets flitting through the dark green foliage of the oaks the long tailed magpies gliding through the trees, the barbet calling insistently from his perch on the top of the deodar.

Forest birds, all of them, they will now be in search of some other stretch of surviving forests. The only visitors will be the crows who have learnt to live with and off humans, and seem to multiply along with roads, houses and people. And even when all the people have gone, the crows will still be there.

Other things to look forward to—trucks thundering past in the night, perhaps a tea and pakora shop around the corner. The grinding of gears, the music of motor horns. Will the whistling thrush be heard above them? The explosions that continually shatter the silence of the mountains as thousand-year-old rocks are dynamited, have frightened away all but the most intrepid of birds

The Vanishing Trees

and animals. Even the bold langurs haven't shown their faces for over a fortnight.

Somehow, I don't think we shall wait for the tea shop to arrive. There must be some other quiet corner, possibly on the next mountain where new roads have yet to come into being. No doubt this is a negative attitude and if I have any sense I'd open my own tea shop. To retreat is to be a loser. But the trees are losers too but when they fall, they do so with a certain dignity.

Never mind. Men come and go, the mountains remain.

The Tenacity of Mountain Water

Early in the summer the grass on the hills is still a pale yellowish green, tinged with brown, and that is how it remains until the monsoon rains bring new life to everything that subsists on the stony Himalayan soil. And then, for four months, the greens are deep and dark and emerald bright.

But the other day, taking a narrow path that left the dry Mussoorie ridge to link up with Pari Tibba (Fairy Hill), I ran across a patch of lush green grass, and I knew there had to be water there.

The grass was soft and springy, spotted with the

The Tenacity of Mountain Water

crimson of small, wild strawberries. Delicate maidenhair, my favorite fern, grew from a cluster of moist, glistening rocks. Moving the ferns a little, I discovered the spring, a freshet of clear sparkling water.

I never cease to wonder at the tenacity of water— its ability to make its way through various strata of rock, zigzagging, backtracking, finding space, cunningly discovering faults and fissures in the mountain, and sometimes travelling underground for great distances before emerging into the open. Of course, there's no stopping water. For no matter how tiny that little trickle, it has to go somewhere!

Like this little spring. At first I thought it was too small to go anywhere... That it would dry up at the edge of the path. Then I discovered that the grass remained soft and green for some distance along the verge, and that there was moisture beneath the grass. This wet stretch ended abruptly; but, on looking further, I saw that it continued on the other side of the path, after briefly going underground again.

I decided to follow its fortunes as it disappeared beneath a tunnel of tall grass and bracken fern. Slithering down a stony slope, I found myself in a small ravine, and there I discovered that my little spring had grown, having been joined by the waters of another spring bubbling up from beneath a patch of primroses.

A short distance away, a spotted forktail stood on a rock, surveying this marriage of the waters. His long, forked tail moved slowly up and down. He paid no attention to me, being totally absorbed in the movements of a water spider. A swift peck, and the spider vanished, completing the bird's breakfast. Thirsty, I cupped my hands and drank a little water. So did the forktail. We had a perennial supply of pure *aqua minerale* all to ourselves!

There was now a rivulet to follow, and I continued down the ravine until I came to a small pool that was fed not only by my brook (I was already thinking of it as my very own!) but also by a little cascade of water coming down from a rocky ledge. I climbed a little way up the rocks and entered a small cave, in which there was just enough space for crouching down. Water dripped and trickled off its roof and sides. And most wonderful of all, some of these drops created tiny rainbows, for a ray of sunlight had struck through a crevice in the cave roof making the droplets of moisture radiant with all the colours of the spectrum.

When I emerged from the cave, I saw a pair of pine martens drinking at the pool. As soon as they saw me, they were up and away, bounding across the ravine and into the trees.

The brook was now a small stream, but I could not follow it much farther, because the hill went into a steep decline and the water tumbled over large, slippery boulders, becoming a waterfall and then a noisy little torrent as it sped towards the valley.

Climbing up the sides of the ravine to the spur of Pari Tibba, I could see the distant silver of a meandering river, and I knew my little stream was destined to become part of it; and that the river would be joined by another that could be seen slipping over the far horizon, and that their combined waters would enter the great Ganga, or Ganges, further downstream.

This mighty river would, in turn, wander over the rich alluvial plains of northern India, finally debouching into the ocean near the Bay of Bengal.

And the ocean, what was it but another droplet in the universe in the greater scheme of things? No greater than the glistening drop of water that helped start it all, where the grass grows greener around my little spring on the mountain.

The Trees are My Brothers

It's good to know that my old friend the jackfruit is finally coming into its own. Apparently it is now much in demand in the West, a fashionable substitute for meat, being used as filling for burgers, sandwiches, pies etc., with one enthusiast even calling it 'mutton hanging from a tree'.

Here in India we have always appreciated a good jackfruit curry, or even better, a jackfruit pickle. I'm a pickle friend myself, and among the twenty different pickles on my sideboard there is always a jar of jackfruit piddle; that's why I call it an old friend. But I had no idea it tasted like mutton. The seed and the pulp have

The Trees are My Brothers

their own individual flavor. As it grows on a tree we call it a fruit, but we cook it as though it were a vegetable. And it, to some, tastes like mutton, then perhaps some meat-eaters will become vegetarians. On the other hand, some vegetarians might not care for its meaty flavor!

When I was a boy, we had an old jackfruit tree growing beside the side verandah. I spent a lot of time in the trees surrounding my grandmother's bungalow, and this one was easy to climb. The others included several guava and lichi trees, lemons and grapefruits, and of course a couple of mango trees—but these last were difficult to climb.

'Why do you spend so much time in the trees?' complained my grandmother. 'Why not do something useful for a change?'

'The trees are my brothers,' I would say, 'I like to play with them.'

And I still think of them as my brothers, although I can no longer climb trees or play in them. But I still think of them as human beings possessed of individuality and charm. Just as no two humans are exactly alike (unless) they happen to be twins), so no two trees are the same. Like humans they grow from seed. They develop branches as arms and leaves like flowing hair. We give birth to children, they give birth to fruits and flowers. We shelter our young, they shelter the small creatures of the forest.

However, unlike us they spring from the soul, from the land—that very land that gives us food and pasture and protection; the land that we so casually take for granted, preferring to build upon it rather than grow upon it. Where will our cattle graze when the last green spaces have gone?

'No problem,' says a young friend. 'We can always import our milk.'

The other day I came across an old book that had been on my shelf for many years. *Farmer's Glory* by A.G. Street, written several decades ago. In his epilogue he writes:

> It is perhaps nothing to boast about, but there is little doubt that the present prosperity of British farming is mainly due to one man, who is now dead. His name was Adolf Hitler. There is no disputing that it was the fear of famine during the early 1940s which taught the British nation that despite all man's cleverness and inventions, when real danger comes an island people must turn for succour to the only permanent asset they possess, the land of their own country. It has never, and will never, let them down; always provided they realize and obey this eternal truth—that to make the land serve man, man must first be content to serve the land.

Surely it is this love of the land and willingness to serve

it that is at the heart of true patriotism. The patriotic songs and speeches that we hear from time to time are fine for stirring up the emotions, but it is really the connect between ourselves and the 'do bigha zameen' on which we grow our fruit and grain that emboldens us to protect it.

I think I am correct in saying that most of our jawans, the young men who join the solid ranks of the Indian Army, come from rural backgrounds; some from the hills, some from the vast plains and hinterland of our country. They know the value of the land. They have grown up in villages and have worked with their families in the rice fields, or sugarcane plantations, or mango-groves, or wheat or corn or mustard or fields of an infinite variety of crops. More than city folk, they know the value of the land—its true worth in terms of either prosperity or poverty. And so they are ready to defend it, to fight for it against all corners. The best soldiers come from the soil that they and their forefathers have tilled.

So let us protect the land—not just from the intruder or the enemy, but also from those who would turn the field or the forest into one more concrete jungle.

Of course there are those who prefer concrete jungles. Like my young friend who wants to live in a Smart City and never mind the cities that are no longer smart. My advice to him (unheeded of course) is to go back to his roots, create a smart little village, and plant jackfruit trees!

Petals on the Ganga

Flowers floating down the river: yellow and scarlet canna lilies, roses, jasmine and hibiscus. They are placed in boats made of broad leaves, then consigned to the water with a prayer. The current carries them swiftly downstream, and they bob about on the water for fifty, sometimes a hundred yards, before being submerged in the river. The Ganga or Ganges issues through a gorge in the mountains with a low booming sound, rushing past the town of Haridwar (Door of Lord Hari, or Vishnu), one of the most sacred of Hindu pilgrim centres.

The river is fast and muddy but this does not deter

thousands of people from descending the steps to the bathing-ghats, and plunging into the cold, snow-fed water. For the Ganga is reputed to wash away all sin. Hindu mythology tells us that the Ganga descended straight from heaven. For a thousand years a devout prince stood with his arms upraised, praying for water to enable him to make the funeral obligations for the ashes of his 60,000 grand-uncles. Almost all the gods were involved in the affair. Finally, when the waters of the Ganga were released from heaven, and the river reached the earth, the Prince mounted his chariot and rode towards the spot where the ashes of his kinsmen lay. Wherever he went, the Ganga meekly followed. Gods, nymphs, demons, giants, sages and great snakes all joined the procession, and as the river hurried on, in the footsteps of the Prince, the whole multitude of created beings bathed in her sacred waters and washed away their sins.

The multitude that followed the Prince could be the same multitude that throngs the riverfront today. I see no one who is not delighted at entering the water. It is a big crowd, although this is just an ordinary day of the week and not an occasion of any religious significance. But for the Hindu every day is a good day for bathing in the Ganga.

At the time of major festivals, such as Baisakhi, which takes place at the commencement of the Hindu solar year (March–April), elaborate arrangements have to be made for the benefit of the great influx of pilgrims who come here from all corners of the country. The number of pilgrims at the Baisakhi festival usually exceeds 100,000. During the Kumbh festival, held every twelve years (when the planet Jupiter is in Aquarius and the sun enters Aries), there may be more than 500,000 present on the great bathing day. This is five times the normal population of Haridwar. And when one realizes that the town is bounded by steep hills on one side, and the river on the other, and has just the one main street leading to the riverfront, the press of people can well be imagined.

Fortunately, the main street is a broad one. I find the road shaded by tall, old peepul and banyan trees. In some places the trees reach right across the street to touch the roots of the tall, old buildings on the other side. At several places, we find young peepul trees growing out of the walls of houses. No one fells the sacred peepul. It is better that a wall should crumble! In a world where trees and forests are rapidly disappearing, this is one tree that will survive, for peepul trees are believed to be the abodes of the spirits and the man who cuts so much as a branch will be pursued by all the demons he has disturbed.

Peepuls will live for hundreds of years, and Haridwar's oldest trees must have been here long before the present town reached maturity. Some will be as old as the 11th century Mayaduri temple, which is probably the oldest temple in Haridwar. On a sultry day, there can no spot more pleasant than the shade of a peepul tree. It is no wonder that the man who plants one of these trees is pleased by generations of Hindus to come. While I stand beneath a peepul, a devout and elderly man approaches with a watering-can, and circling the tree, waters the soil around the base of the tree trunk. I move out of the way of his sprinkler, watching the ritual with some surprise. It has been raining steadily for some days, and the trees had no need for water.

'Why do you water the tree?' I ask.

'Why does one water anything?' asks the man. 'So that it may grow and flourish, of course.'

'But it's been raining almost every day for the past week.'

'Ah, but rain is something else,' he says, 'I am not responsible for the rain. This rain is from the Ganga. It makes a lot of difference.'

I do not argue with him. He waters the tree with love and his love for the tree, as much as rain-water or river-water, is what makes it flourish.

Leaving the main street, I enter the bazaar.

The Haridwar bazaar is a long, narrow winding street, probably the oldest part of the town and free of all vehicular traffic. The road is no more than four yards wide. The smaller shops are spilling over with sweets, pickles, bead necklaces, sacred texts, ritual designs, festival images and bazaar pictures of the gods and gurus in vibrant technicolour. There is something in these naive, gaudy prints that acts as a transformer, making the more abstract philosophies of Hinduism comprehensible to anxious farmers or tired truck drivers.

The bazaar winds and turns back upon itself, and eventually I find myself back at the riverfront, gazing out across the river at the forested foothills. Few of the pilgrims on the bathing-steps can realize that sometimes at night tigers stand on the opposite bank watching the bright illuminations of the temples, or that wild elephants stand listening to the rumbling of the trains bringing pilgrims to Haridwar from all parts of India.

It is evening now, and there are fewer people at the ghats. There is a breeze coming up the river. More flowers are being sold and now the leaf-boats are lit by diyas, wicks dipped in oil. The little boats are swept away, sometimes travelling a considerable distance before being upset by submerged rocks or inquisitive fish. I, too, send an offering downstream, but my boat sails beneath the legs of a late bather, and disappears beneath the pilgrim.

Wild Flowers near a Mountain Stream

Below my house is a forest of oak and maple and Himalayan rhododendron. A path twists its way down through the trees, over an open ridge where red sorrel grows wild, and then steeply down through a tangle of thorn bushes, vines and rangal bamboo. At the bottom of the hill the path leads on to a grassy verge, surrounded by wild rose. A stream runs close by the verge, tumbling over smooth pebbles, over rocks worn yellow with age, on its way to the plains and the little Song River and finally to the sacred Ganges.

When I first discovered the stream it was April and

the wild roses were flowering, small white blossoms lying in clusters. There were primroses on the hill slopes, and an occasional late-flowering rhododendron provided a splash of red against the dark green of the hill.

The St John's Wort was flowering profusely on small shrubs.

Many legends have grown around this flower of pure dazzling sunshine which takes its family name—Hypericaceae—from the great Titan god Hyperion, who was the father of the Greek god of the sun, Apollo.

Is a friend of yours insane? Then get him to drink the sap from the leaves and stalks of the St John's Wort. He will be well again.

Are you hurt? If your wounds do not heal, take the juice and put it on the wound; and if the bleeding will not stop, take more juice.

Is your father bald? Then he must rise early one morning and bathe his head with the dew from St John's Wort, and his hair will grow again.

Do you live on the Isle of Man? Then beware! Tread not on the St John's Wort after sunset, lest a fairy horseman arise and carry you off. He will land you anywhere.

These are all English or Irish superstitions, but the St John's Wort is as profuse in the lower ranges of the Himalayas as it is anywhere in Europe.

Wild Flowers near a Mountain Stream

A spotted forktail, a bird of the Himalayan streams, was much in evidence during those early visits. It moved nimbly over the boulders with a fairy tread, and continually wagged its tail.

In May and June, when the hills are always brown and dry, it remained cool and green near the stream, where ferns and maidenhair and long grasses continued to thrive. Downstream I found a cave with water dripping from the roof, the water spangled gold and silver in the shafts of sunlight that pushed through the slits in the cave roof. Few people came there. Sometimes a milkman or a coal-burner would cross the stream on his way to a village; but the nearby hill station's summer visitors had not discovered this haven of wild and green things.

The monkeys—langurs, with white and silver-grey fur, black faces and long swishing tails—had discovered the place, but they kept to the trees and sunlit slopes. They grew quite accustomed to my presence, and carried on with their work and play as though I did not exist. The young ones scuffled and wrestled like boys, while their parents attended to each other's toilets, stretching themselves out on the grass, beautiful animals with slim waists and long sinewy legs, and tails full of character. They were clean and polite, much nicer than the red monkeys of the plains.

During the rains the stream became a rushing torrent,

bushes and small trees were swept away, and the friendly murmur of the water became a threatening boom. I did not visit the spot very often. There were leeches in the long grass, and they would fasten themselves on to my legs and feast on my blood. But it was always worthwhile tramping through the forest to feast my eyes on the foliage that sprang up in tropical profusion—soft, spongy moss; great stag ferns on the trunks of trees; mysterious and sometimes evil-looking orchids; the climbing convolvulus opening its purple secrets to the morning sun; and the wood sorrel, or oxalis—so named because of the oxalic acid derived from its roots—with its clover-like leaflets, which fold down like umbrellas at the first sign of rain.

And then, after a November hailstorm, it was winter, and one could not lie on the frostbitten grass. The sound of the stream was the same, but I missed the birds.

It snowed—the snow lay heavy on the branches of the oak trees and piled up in the culverts—and the grass and the ferns and wild flowers were pressed to sleep beneath a cold white blanket; but the stream flowed on, pushing its way through and under the whiteness, towards another river, towards another spring.

Of Rivers and Pilgrims

It's a funny thing, but long before I arrive at a place I can usually tell whether I am going to like it or not. Thus, while I was still some twenty miles from the district town of Pauri, I felt it was not going to be my sort of place, and sure enough it wasn't. A seedy, overgrown place, with too many government offices. On the other hand, while Nandprayag was still out of sight, I knew I was going to like it. And I did.

Perhaps, it's something on the wind—emanations of an atmosphere—that carry to me well before I arrive at my destination. I can't really explain it, and of course it's silly to make judgements in advance. But it does happen.

Anyway, I felt I was nearing home as soon as the bus brought me into the cheerful roadside hamlet, a little way above the Nandakini River's confluence with the Alaknanda. A prayag is a meeting place of two rivers, hence Nandprayag, the place where these two mountain rivers meet. As there are many rivers in the Garhwal Himalayas, all linking up to join either the Ganga or the Yamuna, it follows that there are numerous prayags, in themselves places of pilgrimage as well as wayside halts en route to the higher Hindu shrines at Kedarnath and Badrinath. Nowhere else in these mountains are there so many temples, sacred streams, holy places and holy men.

Some little way above Nandprayag's sleepy little bazaar is a tourist rest house. It has a well-kept garden surrounded by fruit trees and is a little distance from the general hubbub of the main road.

Above it is the old pilgrim path. Just over twenty years ago, if you were a pilgrim intent on seeking salvation at the abode of the gods, you travelled on foot all the way from the plains, climbing about 200 miles in a couple of months. Those pilgrims had the time, the faith and the endurance. Illness and misadventure often dogged their footsteps, but what was a little suffering if at the end of the day they arrived at the very portals of heaven?

Today's pilgrims may not be lacking in devotion, but

Of Rivers and Pilgrims

most of them do expect to come home again.

Along the old pilgrim path are several handsome houses, set among mango trees and the fronds of the papaya and banana. Higher up the hill the pine forests commence, but down here it is almost subtropical. Nandprayag is only about 3,000 feet above sea level—a height at which the vegetation is usually lush provided there is protection from the wind.

In one of these double-storeyed houses lives Devki Nandan, a scholar and recluse. He welcomes me into his home and plies me with food till I am close to bursting. He has a great love for this little corner of Garhwal and proudly shows me his collection of cuttings of articles about the area. One is from a travelogue by Sister Nivedita—an Englishwoman, Margaret Noble, who became an interpreter of Hinduism to the West. Visiting Nandprayag in 1928, she wrote:

> Nandprayag is a place that ought to be famous for its beauty and order. For a mile or two before reaching it we had noticed the superior character of the agriculture and even some careful gardening of fruits and vegetables. The peasantry also suddenly grew handsome, not unlike the Kashmiris. The town itself is new, rebuilt since the Gohna flood, and its temple stands far out across the fields on the shore of

> the Prayag. But in this short time a wonderful energy has been at work on architectural carvings and the little place is full of gem-like beauties. As the road crosses the river, I noticed two or three old Pathan tombs, the only traces of Mohammedanism that we had seen north of Srinagar in Garhwal.

Little has changed since Sister Nivedita's visit. There is still a small and thriving Pathan population in Nandprayag. In fact, when I called on Mr Nandan, he was in the act of sending out Eid greetings to his Muslim friends. Some of the old graves have disappeared in the debris from new road cuttings. As for the beautiful temple described by Sister Nivedita, I learned that it had been swept away by a mighty flood in 1970 when a cloudburst and subsequent landslide up-river resulted in great destruction downstream.

Mr Nandan remembers the time when he walked to the small hill station of Pauri to join the old Messmore Christian Mission School, where so many famous sons of Garhwal received their early education. It took him four days marching to get to Pauri. Now it is just four hours by bus. It was only after the Chinese invasion of 1962 that there was a sudden spurt in road building in the northern hill districts. Before that, everyone walked and thought nothing of it.

Of Rivers and Pilgrims

Sitting on my own that same evening in the little garden of the rest house, I heard innumerable birds break into song. I did not see them, because the light was fading and the trees were dark; but I heard the rather melancholy call of the hill dove, the ascending trill of the koel, and much shrieking, whistling, and twittering that I could not assign to any particular species.

Now, once again, while I sit on the lawn surrounded by zinnias in full bloom, I am teased by that feeling of having been here before, on this lush hillside, among the pomegranates and oleanders. Is it some childhood memory asserting itself? As far as I know, I never travelled in these parts.

It's true that Nandprayag resembles some parts of the Doon Valley (where I grew up) before the Doon was submerged by a tidal wave of humanity. But in the Doon there is no great river running past your garden. Here there are two, and they are also part of this feeling of belonging.

Presently, the room boy joins me for a chat on the lawn. He is in fact running the rest house in the absence of the manager. Wherever I go in India, the manager is usually absent; it seems to make no difference. A coach load of pilgrims is due at any moment, but until they arrive the place is empty and only the birds can be heard.

The room boy's name is Janakpal and he tells me

something about his village on the next mountain, where a marauding leopard has been carrying off goats and cattle. He doesn't think much of the laws protecting leopards—nothing can be done unless the animal becomes a man-eater.

A shower of rain descends on us, and so do the pilgrims. Janakpal leaves me to attend to his duties. But I am not left alone for long. A youngster with a cup of tea is the next to interview me. He wants me to take him to Mussoorie or New Delhi. He is fed up, he says, with washing dishes here.

'You are better off here,' I tell him sincerely. 'In Mussoorie you will have twice as many dishes to wash. In Delhi, ten times as many.'

'Yes, but there are cinemas and video and TV there,' he says, leaving me without an argument. Bird song may have charms for me, but not for the restless dishwasher in tranquil Nandprayag.

The rain stops and I go for a walk. The pilgrims keep to themselves, but the locals are always ready to talk. I remember a saying (and it may have originated in these hills), which goes: 'All men are my friends. I have only to meet them.' In Nandprayag, where life still moves at a leisurely and civilized pace, one is constantly meeting them.

The Joy of Water

Each drop represents a little bit of creation-and of life itself. When the monsoon brings to northern India the first rains of summer, the parched earth opens its pores and quenches its thirst with a hiss of ecstasy. After baking in the sun for the last few months, the land looks cracked, dusty and tired. Now, almost overnight, new grass springs up, there is renewal everywhere, and the damp earth releases a fragrance sweeter than any devised by man.

Water brings joy to earth, grass, leaf-bud, blossom, insect, bird, animal and the pounding heart of man. Small children run out of their homes to romp naked in the rain. Buffaloes, which have spent the summer listlessly around lakes gone dry, now plunge into a heaven of muddy water. Soon the lakes and rivers will overflow with the monsoon's generosity. Trekking in the Himalayan foothills, I recently walked for kilometres without encountering habitation. I was just scolding myself for not having brought along a water bottle, when I came across a patch of green on a rock face. I parted a curtain of tender maidenhair fern and discovered a tiny spring issuing from the rock-nectar for the thirsty traveller.

I stayed there for hours, watching the water descend, drop by drop, into a tiny casement in the rocks. Each drop reflected creation. That same spring, I later discovered, joined other springs to form a swift, tumbling stream, which went cascading down the hill into other streams until, in the plains, it became part of a river. And that river flowed into another mightier river that kilometres later emptied into the ocean. Be like water, taught Lao-tzu, philosopher and founder of Taoism. Soft and limpid, it finds its way through, over or under any obstacle. It does not quarrel; it simply moves on.

A small pool in the rocks outside my cottage in the Mussoorie hills, provides me endless delight. Water beetles paddle the surface, while tiny fish lurk in the shallows. Sometimes a spotted forktail comes to drink, hopping delicately from rock to rock. And once I saw a barking deer, head lowered at the edge of the pool. I stood very still, anxious that it should drink its fill. It did, and then, looking up, saw me and leapt across the ravine to disappear into the forest.

In summer the pool is almost dry. Even this morning, there was just enough water for the fish and tadpoles to survive. But as I write, there is a pattering on the tin roof of the cottage, and I look out to see the raindrops pitting the surface of the pool.

Tomorrow the spotted forktail will be back. Perhaps the barking deer will return. I open the window wide and allow the fragrance of the rain and freshened earth to waft into my room.

Sounds I Like to Hear

All night the rain has been drumming on the corrugated tin roof. There has been no storm, no thunder just the steady swish of a tropical downpour. It helps one to lie awake; at the same time, it doesn't keep one from sleeping.

It is a good sound to read by the rain outside, the quiet within—and, although tin roofs are given to springing unaccountable leaks, there is in general a feeling of being untouched by, and yet in touch with, the rain.

Gentle rain on a tin roof is one of my favourite sounds. And early in the morning, when the rain has stopped, there are other sounds I like to hear—a crow shaking the raindrops from his feathers and cawing rather disconsolately; babblers and bulbuls bustling in and out of bushes and long grass in search of worms and insects; the sweet, ascending trill of the Himalayan whistling-thrush; dogs rushing through damp undergrowth.

A cherry tree, bowed down by the heavy rain, suddenly rights itself, flinging pellets of water in my face.

Some of the best sounds are made by water. The water of a mountain stream, always in a hurry, bubbling over rocks and chattering, 'I'm late, I'm late!' like the White Rabbit, tumbling over itself in its anxiety to reach the bottom of the hill, the sound of the sea, especially when it is far away—or when you hear it by putting a sea shell to your ear. The sound made by dry and thirsty earth, as it sucks at a sprinkling of water. Or the sound of a child drinking thirstily the water running down his chin and throat.

Water gushing out of the pans of an old well outside a village while a camel moves silently round the well. Bullock-cart wheels creaking over rough country roads. The clip-clop of a pony carriage, and the tinkle of its bell, and the singsong call of its driver...

Bells in the hills. A schoolbell ringing, and children's voices drifting through an open window. A temple-bell, heard faintly from across the valley. Heavy silver ankle-bells on the feet of sturdy hill women. Sheep bells heard high up on the mountainside.

Do falling petals make a sound? Just the tiniest and softest of sounds, like the drift of falling snow. Of course big flowers, like dahlias, drop their petals with a very definite flop. These are showoffs, like the hawk-moth who comes flapping into the rooms at night instead of emulating the butterfly dipping lazily on the afternoon breeze.

One must return to the birds for favourite sounds, and the birds of the plains differ from the birds of the hills. On a cold winter morning in the plains of northern India, if you walk some way into the jungle you will hear the familiar call of the black partridge: *Bhagwan teri giedrat* it seems to cry, which means: 'Oh God! Great is thy might.'

The cry rises from the bushes in all directions; but an hour later not a bird is to be seen or heard and the jungle is so very still that the silence seems to shout at you.

There are sounds that come from a distance, beautiful because they are far away, voices on the wind—they 'walketh upon the wings of the wind'. The cries of fishermen out on the river. Drums beating rhythmically in a distant village. The croaking of frogs from the rainwater pond behind the house. I mean frogs at a distance. A frog croaking beneath one's window is as welcome as a motor horn.

But some people like motor horns. I know a taxi-driver who never misses an opportunity to use his horn. It was made to his own specifications, and it gives out a resonant bugle-call. He never tires of using it. Cyclists and pedestrians always scatter at his approach. Other cars veer off the road. He is proud of his horn. He loves its strident sound, which only goes to show that some men's sounds are other men's noises!

Homely sounds, though we don't often think about them, are the ones we miss most when they are gone. A kettle on the boil. A door that creaks on its hinges. Old sofa springs. Familiar voices lighting up the dark. Ducks quacking in the rain.

And so we return to the rain, with which my favourite sounds began.

I have sat out in the open at night, after a shower of rain when the whole air is murmuring and tinkling with the voices of crickets and grasshoppers and little frogs. There is one melodious sound, a sweet repeated trill, which I have never been able to trace to its source. Perhaps it is a little tree frog. Or it may be a small green cricket. I shall never know.

I am not sure that I really want to know. In an age when a scientific and rational explanation has been given for almost everything we see and touch and hear, it is good to be left with one small mystery, a mystery sweet and satisfying and entirely my own.

Listen!

Listen to the night wind in the trees,
Listen to the summer grass singing;
Listen to the time that's tripping by,
And the dawn dew falling.
Listen to the moon as it climbs the sky,
Listen to the pebbles humming;
Listen to the mist in the trembling leaves,
And the silence calling.

Guests Who Fly in from the Forest

When mist fills the Himalayan valleys, and heavy monsoon rain sweeps across the hills, it is natural for wild creatures to seek shelter. Any shelter is welcome in a storm—and sometimes my cottage in the forest is the most convenient refuge.

There is no doubt that I make things easier for all concerned by leaving most of my windows open—I am one of those peculiar people who like to have plenty of fresh air indoors—and if a few birds, beasts and insects come in too, they're welcome, provided they don't make too much of a nuisance of themselves.

I must confess that I did lose patience with a bamboo beetle who blundered in the other night and fell into the water jug. I rescued him and pushed him out of the window. A few seconds later he came whirring in again, and with unerring accuracy landed with a plop in the same jug. I fished him out once more and offered him the freedom of the night. But attracted no doubt by the light and warmth of my small sitting-room, he came buzzing back, circling the room like a helicopter looking for a good place to land. Quickly I covered the water jug. He landed in a bowl of wild dahlias, and I allowed him to remain there, comfortably curled up in the hollow of a flower.

Sometimes, during the day, a bird visits me—a deep purple whistling-thrush, hopping about on long dainty legs, peering to right and left, too nervous to sing. She perches on the windowsill, looking out at the rain. She does not permit any familiarity. But if I sit quietly in my chair, she will sit quietly on her windowsill, glancing quickly at me now and then just to make sure that I'm keeping my distance. When the rain stops, she glides away, and it is only then, confident in her freedom, that she bursts into full-throated song, her broken but haunting melody echoing down the ravine.

A squirrel comes sometimes, when his home in the oak tree gets waterlogged. Apparently he is a bachelor;

anyway, he lives alone. He knows me well, this squirrel, and is bold enough to climb on to the dining-table looking for tidbits which he always finds, because I leave them there deliberately. Had I met him when he was a youngster, he would have learned to eat from my hand; but I have only been here a few months. I like it this way. I am not looking for pets: these are simply guests.

Last week, as I was sitting down at my desk to write a long-deferred article, I was startled to see an emerald-green praying mantis sitting on my writing pad. He peered up at me with his protruberant glass bead eyes, and I stared down at him through my reading glasses. When I gave him a prod, he moved off in a leisurely way. Later I found him examining the binding of Whitman's *Leaves of Grass*; perhaps he had found a succulent bookworm. He disappeared for a couple of days, and then I found him on the dressing-table, preening himself before the mirror. Perhaps I am doing him an injustice in assuming that he was preening. Maybe he thought he'd met another mantis and was simply trying to make contact. Anyway, he seemed fascinated by his reflection.

Out in the garden, I spotted another mantis, perched on the jasmine bush. Its arms were raised like a boxer's. Perhaps they're a pair, I thought, and went indoors and fetched my mantis and placed him on the jasmine bush, opposite his fellow insect. He did not like what he saw—

no comparison with his own image!—and made off in a huff.

My most interesting visitor comes at night, when the lights are still burning—a tiny bat who prefers to fly in at the door, should it be open, and will use the window only if there's no alternative. His object in entering the house is to snap up the moths that cluster around the lamps.

All the bats I've seen fly fairly high, keeping near the ceiling as far as possible, and only descending to ear level (my ear level) when they must; but this particular bat flies in low, like a dive bomber, and does acrobatics amongst the furniture, zooming in and out of chair legs and under tables. Once, while careening about the room in this fashion, he passed straight between my legs.

Has his radar gone wrong, I wondered, or is he just plain crazy?

I went to my shelves of *Natural History* and looked up Bats, but could find no explanation for this erratic behaviour. As a last resort, I turned to an ancient volume, Sterndale's *Indian Mammalia* (Calcutta, 1884), and in it, to my delight, I found what I was looking for—

> ...a bat found near Mussoorie by Captain Hutton, on the southern range of hills at 5,500 feet; head and body, 1.4 inch; skims close to the ground, instead of

flying high as bats generally do, Habitat, Jharipani, N.W. Himalayas.

Apparently the bat was rare even in 1884.

Perhaps I've come across one of the few surviving members of the species: Jharipani is only two miles from where I live. And I feel rather offended that modern authorities should have ignored this tiny bat; possibly they feel that it is already extinct. If so, I'm pleased to have rediscovered it. I am happy that it survives in my small corner of the woods, and I undertake to celebrate it in prose and verse.

In Search of a Winter Garden

If someone were to ask me to choose between writing an essay on the Taj Mahal or on the last rose of summer, I'd take the rose—even if it was down to its last petal. Beautiful, cold, white marble leaves me—well, just a little cold.

Roses are warm and fragrant, and almost every flower I know, wild or cultivated, has its own unique quality, whether it be subtle fragrance or arresting colour or loveliness of design. Unfortunately, winter has come to the Himalayas, and the hillsides are now brown and dry, the only colour being that of the red sorrel growing

In Search of a Winter Garden

from the limestone rocks. Even my small garden looks rather forlorn, with the year's last darkeyed nasturtium looking every bit like the Lone Ranger surveying the surrounding wilderness from his saddle. The marigolds have dried in the sun, and tomorrow I will gather the seed. The beanstalk that grew rampant during the monsoon is now down to a few yellow leaves and empty bean pods.

'This won't do,' I told myself the other day. 'I must have flowers!'

Prem, who had been down to the valley town of Dehra the previous week, had made me even more restless, because he had spoken of masses of sweet peas in full bloom in the garden of one of the town's public schools. Down in the plains, winter is the best time for gardens, and I remembered my grandmother's house in Dehra, with its long rows of hollyhocks, neatly staked sweet peas, and beds ablaze with red salvia and antirrhinum. Neither Grandmother nor the house are there anymore, but surely there are other beautiful gardens, I mused, and maybe I could visit the school where Prem had seen the sweet peas. It was a long time since I had enjoyed their delicate fragrance.

So I took the bus down the hill, and throughout the two-hour journey I dozed and dreamt of gardens—cottage gardens in the English countryside, tropical gardens in Florida, Mughal gardens in Kashmir, the Hanging Gardens of Babylon! What had they really been like, I wondered.

And then we were in Dehra, and I got down from the bus and walked down the dusty, busy road to the school Prem had told me about.

It was encircled by a high wall, and, tiptoeing, I could see playing fields and extensive school buildings and, in the far distance, a dollop of colour that *may* have been a garden. Prem's eyesight was obviously better than mine!

I made my way to a wrought-iron gate that would have done justice to a medieval fortress, and found it chained and locked. On the other side stood a tough-looking guard, with a rifle.

'May I enter?' I asked.

'Sorry, sir. Today is holiday. No school today.'

'I don't want to attend classes. I want to see sweet peas.'

'Kitchen is on the other side of the ground.'

'Not green peas. Sweet peas. I'm looking for the garden.'

'I am guard here.'

'*Garden.*'

'No garden, only guard.'

I tried telling him that I was an old boy of the school and that I was visiting the town after a long interval. This

In Search of a Winter Garden

was true up to a point, because I had once been admitted to this very school, and after one day's attendance had insisted on going back to my old school. The guard was unimpressed. And perhaps it was poetic justice that the gates were barred to me now.

Disconsolate, I strolled down the main road, past a garage, a cinema, and a row of eating houses and tea shops. Behind the shops there seemed to be a park of sorts, but you couldn't see much of it from the road because of the buildings, the press of people, and the passing trucks and buses. But I found the entrance, unbarred this time, and struggled through patches of overgrown shrubbery until, like Alice after finding the golden key to the little door in the wall, I looked upon a lovely little garden.

There were no sweet peas, and the small fountain was dry. But around it, filling a large circular bed, were masses of bright yellow California poppies.

They stood out like sunshine after rain, and my heart leapt as Wordsworth's must have, when he saw his daffodils. I found myself oblivious to the sounds of the bazaar and the road, just as the people outside seemed oblivious to this little garden. It was as though it had been waiting here all this time, waiting for me to come by and discover it.

I am fortunate. Something like this is always

happening to me. As Grandmother often said, 'When one door closes, another door opens.' And while one gate had been closed upon the sweet peas, another had opened on California poppies.